THE YAKUSHIMA GUIDE

Yakumnkey

Published in March 2017 by Mangrove Press, UK.

ISBN: 978-0-9561507-7-6

Mangrove Press
Martello House
2 Western Road
Poole, UK

info@mangrovepress.com
www.mangrovepress.com

CONTENTS

1. INTRODUCTION

It is now 10 years since I started writing the first paperback edition of the Yakumonkey Guide. Back then I had no idea that it would become as popular as it has become and that I might be publishing the third edition ten years down the road. If I look back at the Yakushima that existed then, it is very different to what it is now. When the first edition came out, there was serious worry that Yakushima would not be able to withstand the hordes of tourists that were increasing massively year on year. They were seemingly unstoppable and were threatening the very ecosystem that made Yakushima so unique. But then the world financial crisis hit. And then the natural disasters first in the north and then in the south. One after the other. And the Japanese tourists just stopped coming in the same numbers. This has meant that some businesses have collapsed and yet others have flourished and that there had to be a new market for them to orientate themselves. The curious thing is that while the Japanese tourist numbers slumped, foreign tourists have been increasing at a steady rate, especially from Japan's immediate neighbours like China and South Korea. This has meant that more and more local businesses have had to cater for this blossoming market. The demands of foreign tourists are not the same as those of Japanese and the changes are palpable. Many hotels and hostels now provide websites in English and there are even materials coming out of Yakushima Town Council aimed at foreign tourists.

There is still however so much more to be done. And when you visit you will probably find Yakushima just as baffling as it has always been. This is of course part of its charm. It is like a time capsule to quieter days before the 21st century took us by the throat and throttled us by technology. You will find that for the majority of people who live on Yakushima, life is how it always was. It is now and it has always been about survival. About people and community. About the connection to nature and weather systems with many people living off the land and the tourists who visit.

Be aware that Yakushima is still one of the least wealthy areas of Japan. Nowadays tourism is the island's largest economy with an estimated income of 10 billion yen a year but unfortunately the wealth of mainland tourists has not filtered down to the native islanders. With average incomes still at ¥3 million a year (70% of the national average) and average hourly pay at just ¥650 an hour, many people struggle to make a living. I have therefore tried to include as many local businesses as I could when making this guide and urge you to use smaller Yakushima-based businesses during your stay. Some of these speak little English (those that do I indicate in the guide) but Yakushima is generally a friendly place willing to help and with good humour and persistence most things can be accomplished. Should you need a little help with your Japanese, however, I have included the Japanese words in their original form to aid in communication (you can point to the word!) and to enable you to read signs.

As far as the physical island goes, it is just the same. The forests are still filled with the same ancient cedar trees so astonishingly old that they were saplings at the birth of the Roman Empire. It still rains heavily high in the mountains creating spectacular waterfalls and crystal clear water so clean it is drinkable straight from source. Wild macaques and deer still roam the mountains in large numbers as they have done for millennia. Species so rare that they only live wild on Yakushima and nowhere else on the planet. But Yakushima is more than any one sight or any one natural phenomena, it is a living, breathing island so full of life that to walk its trails, to touch its greenery and to breathe its air is an affirmation of nature and our place within it. There is nowhere quite like it in the world and its status as a Japanese National Park and a World Natural World Heritage site reflects this rare beauty.

This guide is based on my personal knowledge of Yakushima, having lived and worked there both as a fisherman and a wood craftsman. This allows me to draw on a little local knowledge to let you get the best out of visiting and you will find stories and anecdotes throughout the guide book, some of which are mine and some of which are from the wonderful people who live there.

In this edition of the book I decided it was time to code and colour the trails to make referencing easier. You will now see that the Yodogawa

Trail is light purple and is referred to as Y1 and the Arakawa Trail is dark green as is A1 and so on. Hopefully this will make the trails and the relationships between them much clearer.

The hiking details in this guide include all the main trails. There are many other trails dotted around the island, some of which I refer to in this book, but for the sake of the forest I have not included them in this guide. All of the hiking times I have included are estimates and based on a fairly fit person carrying a backpack, please be on the conservative side when planning routes and take account of gradient and weather conditions in conjunction with a proper hiking map. I recommend that instead of pushing on huge distances in one day that you take your time amongst the trees and open your senses to the forest. It is too special a place to rush through. I hope these pages help you to enjoy the wonders of Yakushima.

Clive Witham

Visit yakumonkey.com for updates on visiting Yakushima

2 THE BASICS

Yakushima is 60 km south of Kyushu Island and at the northern end of the Ryukyu island chain which leads on to Okinawa. On a clear day especially after rain has fallen around the coast, the mountains that make up Cape Sata, the furthest point of mainland Kyushu, are clearly outlined on the northern horizon.

Across the Vincennes Strait to the East is **Tanegashima** (種子島), a relatively flat island, home to Japan's Space exploration program. And to the North West a small volcanic island, only 12 km away, known as **Kuchinoerabu** (口永良部島), and which last erupted in 2015.

Visually the island is impressive. There are over 45 mountain peaks squeezed into a total area of 505 km² which makes it look, at least from the sea, like a botanical castle floating in a Miyazaki animation. The mountain ranges are high with the tallest peak on the island, Miyanoura dake, rising to 1935 m, making it the tallest mountain in all of southern Japan.

The average altitude of the island is 600 m and as most of it is sloping downwards, there are very few places where the land is completely flat. If you stand at the coast and look inwards to the mountains, they appear to form a massive impenetrable wall all the way round its 132 km circumference.

The island was formed around 14 million years ago when granite base-rock was forced up by seismic activity, a process which has never really halted, and it is still rising at a rate of one meter per 1,000 years. While there is some sandstone and shale at the foot of the central mountains, Yakushima is essentially one giant lump of granite.

Hard and solid granite rocks weather slowly and only produce a small amount of soil, and in theory would not be an ideal environment for plants to thrive, but just a glimpse of any photo of the island will tell you that in Yakushima, it is quite the opposite.

THE FLORA

Virtually the whole island is covered in plant life with the state forestry owning a massive 95.5% of Yakushima. And it is here, within the green canopy that covers Yakushima's mountains that the unique qualities of the island really come to bear.

A remarkable variety of plants inhabit the island. There are more than 1,900 species and subspecies distributed gradually up the mountain slopes. There are sub-tropical plants, such as banyan trees near the coast, and then a little higher, warm temperate plants such as chinquapin and evergreen oaks. These then give way to temperate zone plants, such as fir and cypress trees as the mountains rise and ultimately as the tree-line is passed to sub alpine plants such as the Yakushima dwarf bamboo and the famous Yakushima rhododendron. According to UNESCO, the range of vegetation across the island from the coast to the high altitude summits is considered to be the widest not only in Japan but in the whole of East Asia.

This unique forest ecosystem in Yakushima is positioned at the extreme end of the natural distribution of many species. It has over 200 species that are at their southern limit of natural distribution, and equally many identified species that are at their very northernmost point. Yakushima acts as a melting pot between northern and southern species allowing an environment where the two can successfully co-exist and unsurprisingly this has resulted in 94 endemic species only found on the island. With a permanently damp micro-climate, it is also home to an astonishing 300 species of fern and 600 varieties of mosses.

As if this was not enough, there is a particular native species considered so rare that it has been awarded 'Special Natural Monument' status in Japan and which has come to symbolize the natural importance of the island. These are the Japanese cedar trees known as '**Yakusugi**', each over 1,000 years of age, and found somewhere between 600 m and 1800 m on the mountain slopes. They are very large evergreen trees with a dark reddish brown bark and although often referred to as 'cedar' trees in English, 'Sugi' (Crytomeria japonica) actually belong to the cypress family of trees. The wood has a slight red tinge to it, gives off a very distinctive scent and is renowned for its strength and water resistance.

Indeed it was this point that caused them, until very recently, to be almost logged out of existence.

THE FOREST

The cedar forests of Yakushima have a long history of being plundered for the needs of an ever growing Japan. The first records date back to the middle ages when, in the 16th century, forestry surveys of the island were made on the orders of **Hideyoshi Toyotomi** (1537-1598), the great feudal lord and unifier of Japan, who had an eye on using Yakusugi timber in the construction of the Colossal Hall of the Great Buddha of Hokoji Temple in Higashiyama, Kyoto in 1586. In the end it was never used for the temple but it was used in many other structures, including Osumi Sho-hachimangu Shrine (which is now Kagoshima Shrine).

During the Edo period (1603-1868), and under the watchful eye of an eager Lord Shimazu, of the powerful Satsuma clan in Kyushu, the cutting was very selective and only relatively straight standing trees began. It is said that **Jochiku Tomari** (泊如竹) (1570-1655), a Confucianist scholar born in Anbo, had suggested the idea to Shimazu personally and had then persuaded a reluctant island population to agree to cutting down their sacred forests.

The attraction of Yakusugi was that it was both strong and waterproof, making it perfect material to produce the short rectangular roof tiles needed for construction throughout Japan. Each tile had to be 50 cm long, 10 cm wide and 7 mm thick and became the currency of the island's annual tribute to the Satsuma clan. The demand was great in the markets of Osaka and the logging was so intensive that it is believed that over half of the Yakusugi trees were felled and that only around 1,000 long-lived Yakusugi were left standing.

Evidence of Edo period logging activities is all around when wandering through the forests even today. The trail leading up from Kusugawa village known as the Kusugawa Trail (K1) was originally laid for Edo period forest labourers who had to live and work in the forests for extended periods of time, using simple axes to fell the giant cedars. It was sometimes only after the tree had been cut down that it was decided whether or not to use its wood and many great trees still lay fallen, untouched and still intact on the forest floor.

It was not until the Meiji period (1868-1912) that the first signs of de facto conservation were seen when in 1885 the island's forests were placed into the possession of the state. Despite a long legal battle started in 1904 by Yakushima islanders who saw their forestry livelihood under threat, the state owned forest was confirmed in 1920 and the modern era of logging began.

The first conservation measure was the designation of an Academic Reference Forest Reserve in the national forest and in 1924, it became a Heritage Area known as the 'Yakushima Old Growth Japanese Cedar Forest Natural Monument' (the designation was changed to Special Natural Monument in 1954).

However, despite the rudimentary attempts at protection, logging was well underway. In 1923 the forest path from Anbo to Kosugidani was completed and District Forestry offices set up. By the late 1950s, there was a movement to increase the logging of national parks throughout Japan to ease the demand for building materials in post war reconstruction. Logging was therefore extended to the broad leaved forest as well as the Yakusugi and operations intensified considerably especially after the introduction of the chain saw in 1956.

The trees were brought swiftly down the mountains on one of four forest rail tracks. Only one survives today (from Anbo) and is the only active logging rail track in all of Japan. Pictures in Yakusugi museum show forest workers perched on top of several trunks strapped to an engine-less wagon and with controls not unlike the reins of horse, hurtling down the mountain. Not a job for the faint of heart. Nowadays the trucks have engines and can often be seen at the logging station at Arakawa Trail Entrance.

Further signs of conservation came again in 1964 when the area was incorporated into the **Kirishima-Yaku National Park** (霧島屋久国立公園), but logging continued until national forestry priorities began to change from production to more progressive ideas of development and conservation in the 1960s and it was finally halted as recently as in 1971. It then swiftly became an official Wilderness Area and in the 1980s the national park was expanded with 19,000 hectares declared a Biosphere Reserve under the UNESCO Man and Biosphere Program. More protection then came with the creation of The Forest Ecosystem Reserve in 1991 and in December 1993 the awarding of UNESCO World Natural Heritage Site to Yakushima brought 10,747 hectares of the 50,000 hectares of the total area of Yakushima (21%) under international protection.

This collection of protected areas effectively means that activities which may threaten the 'integrity' of the area, such as building, felling trees or bamboo, collecting animals and plants, collecting soil, stones, rocks, fallen leaves and branches, and building fires are prohibited within the Wilderness Area and allowed only under permit in the Special Protection zone of the National Park and Preservation zone of the National Forest.

More recently, coastal areas have finally come under international protection with Nagata beach designated a Wetland of International Importance under the Ramsar Convention in 2005 in recognition of its unique position in the nesting of loggerhead turtles.

Management of the World Heritage area is split between the Environment Agency, the Forestry agency, the Agency for Cultural Affairs and Kagoshima Prefecture. To try to simplify working together the Yakushima World Heritage Area Liaison Committee was formed between them but in reality the problems that Yakushima now faces are exacerbated by a lack of unified administrative control. The sheer numbers of visitors to Yakushima have put a major strain on the island's eco-system with soil erosion and waste management at the forefront.

So far there have been signs that something is being done against the onslaught of tourists on the forests: access to the Arakawa Trail head has now been permanently restricted to private cars and a new system of bio-toilets have been set up. However because there are so many organisations which have to agree before being implemented, change is slow.

The protection of Yakushima is chronically underfunded on a national level and essentially relies on the volunteer work of local people, many of whom neither have the time nor resources to make an effective impact. It is now a fairly regular annual task for locals to climb up to the toilets at Takatsuka mountain hut and carry the contents of the pit latrines down the mountain. Toilets are a major issue as demand exceeds supply and subsequent contamination from pit toilets is causing environmental damage in the areas most needed of protection.

There are further problems in that the mountain huts become so congested in high season that hikers are forced to erect tents around the site, damaging the fragile eco-system. It has been suggested that tourist numbers should be controlled and path closures and other measures need to be implemented to protect the island but, under the current system of management, it appears that change will be very slow.

THE TREES

KIGEN SUGI (紀元杉)

Height: 19.5 m
Trunk circumference: 8.1 m
Age: 3,000 years old
Access: On the mountain road to
Yodogawa Trail Entrance (Y1)

This is one of the most accessible ancient Yakusugi trees as it is quite literally beside the road. It is not only one tree but the host of a variety of other species of trees and plants that live on its weathered body. These include Hinoki cypress, Yamaguruma and Hikagetsutsuji. It also displays the blossoms of Yakushima Rhododendron in early summer.

BUDDHA SUGI (仏陀杉)

Height: 21.5 m
Trunk circumference: 8.0 m
Age: 1,800 years old
Access: Yakusugiland (Y3)

This famous Yakusugi has a clump on its trunk which when seen from a certain angle is supposed to resemble to face of Buddha. It is very weak at its lower trunk with much of it hollow and visitors are restricted by the viewing platform 2 m from the tree for its protection. This has stood since 1997 when attempts to save the tree were put in place including improving soil quality, draining excess water and restricting access. Its upper branches appear full of life with 12 species of epiphyte living and blooming on its trunk including Azaleas, Rhododendrons and Mountain ash.

YAYOI SUGI (弥生杉)

Height: 26.1 m
Trunk circumference: 8.1 m
Age: 3,000 years old
Access: Shiratani Unsuikyo (S1)

The name of this grand old Yakusugi gives us clues about its age. The Yayoi period in Japanese history was between 500 BC and 300 AD and directly followed the Jomon period. It has an odd shape which probably saved it from being felled by Edo period loggers. It is much lower in altitude than many of the other old Yakusugi trees standing at just 710 m above Miyanoura village and common to many of the great Yakusugi, it has ten different epiphyte species growing from the surface of its trunk including Yakushima Rhododendron, Japanese Rowan and Japan Wood-oil.

JOMON SUGI (縄文杉)

Height: 25.3 m
Diameter: 5.22 m
Trunk circumference: 16.4 m
Age: 2,600 - 7,200 years old
Access: Okabu Trail (O1)

This is the granddaddy of them all. It was probably due to its rough and weathered exterior that this magnificent tree managed to survive the extensive logging activities of the Edo period. It was actually called Oiwa sugi (大岩杉) up until 1966 when a local man named Teiji Iwakawa (岩川貞次) bought it national attention. It was then renamed 'Jomon sugi' because initial tests dated it back to the Jomon era (14,000 - 400 BC) and also the fact that the branches appeared to have a similar shape to traditional Jomon earthenware. On its weather-beaten, leathery trunk 13 different species of plant life grow, including Rhododendron, Trochodendron and Mountain Ash.

THE FAUNA

Since Yakushima separated from the Kyushu mainland some 15,000 years ago, the environment of the island has produced a rich and quasi-primitive habitat. There are various subspecies that are endemic to Yakushima, the most well-known of which the Yaku-macaques and the Yaku-dear. There are also 167 bird species, 14 species of reptiles, 8 species of amphibians, and approximately 1,900 species of insects which have been confirmed to inhabit Yakushima, making this small island extremely abundant in fauna.

YAKU MACAQUES (ヤクザル) Macaca fuscata yakui

This subspecies of the Japanese Macaque can only be found in the wild on Yakushima Island. They are fairly short and stout compared to their mainland cousins, at an average height of 50 cm and weight of 10 kg, and their fur is longer and thicker.

Estimates on their numbers lie at around 6,000 and as they roam freely on the mountains mostly in small groups of four to five, can often be seen in the forest, near the main road and sometimes in the villages.

The macaques have the freedom of the island but are frequently found in the laurel forests where there are berry-bearing trees. They spend their days foraging, grooming and carefully picking bugs from each other's fur. Their diet consists mainly of berries from bayberry (ヤマモモ) and Japanese fig (イヌビワ) plants in early summer and acorns (ドングリ) in autumn/winter. They are, however, far from fussy and eat over a hundred different types of plants as well as mushrooms (キノコ) and insects.

If you come across a troop, they usually scamper away. But sometimes if you keep your head down and avoid eye contact, they will ignore you and allow you to observe them. The babies (born in the spring after the snow has thawed) are especially curious. They are invariably with their mothers, often riding on their backs for up to a year.

There are many places you may come across macaques. They can often be seen loitering at the roadside on the road to Yakusugiland, particularly early morning and late afternoon. They are of course waiting for passing tourists to throw them food, who despite the signs saying otherwise, get so excited at seeing them that they throw all kinds of junk out of the window with amazing consistency. This familiarity with human food sources has led to all kinds of problems with local people.

For many of the farmers on the island, the monkeys are little more than pests who destroy their crops on a regular basis. Ponkan and Tankan citrus fruit, both of which resemble small oranges, are a favorite of the macaques and there has been a battle raging between them and the farmers for many years. In 1989, as much as ¥10 million was recorded in damage from macaques in the north part of the island. It is now common to see electric fences surrounding the citrus groves to prevent damage but this kind of protection is expensive and a large number of monkeys are captured and killed, either by professional hunters or in crude farmers' traps.

YAKU SHIKA DEER (ヤクシカ) Cervus nippon yakushimae

The Yakushika are another subspecies of the mainland deer. They number around 7,000 and are a common sight in the mountains. Like the macaques they are smaller than the mainland species. They can often be seen following troops of macaques and scavenging on the fruit they drop from the trees.

The Yakushika are another subspecies of the mainland deer. They number around 7,000 and are a common sight in the mountains. Like the macaques they are smaller than the main-  land species. They can often be seen following troops of macaques and scavenging on the fruit they drop from the trees.

They used to hold a spiritual place in the beliefs of islanders who traditionally held them to be the messengers of 'Ippon Hoju Daigongen', the God of the mountain. That belief is no longer widely held and although officially protected, there is now an annual hunting season and, like the macaques, farmers trap them as pests on their land. It is not just the locals however who have problems with the deer.

Environmentalists wishing to protect the rare plants and trees on Yakushima have found that their efforts at conservation have mostly been eaten by ever increasing numbers of deer. Research is being carried out at present as to the extent of this destruction by fencing off key areas of forest and comparing these with the growth of the unfenced areas around them and some kind of balance is sought between the continued presence of deer and the flora of the forest.

OTHER MAMMALS

Other mammals, none of which you are likely to see on a short visit, include the Siberian weasel, Japanese mole, Small/ Large Japanese field mouse, Horseshoe bat and the unfortunate recent introduction of Raccoon dogs to Yakushima's fragile natural habitat.

INSECTS

If you walk through the forests of Yakushima, you cannot fail but notice that it is alive with insects of all shapes and sizes. Despite their often strange appearance most are perfectly harmless, but of the 19,000 species of insects living on Yakushima, there are a handful that needs to be treated with caution.

MUKADE (百足) are large reddish brown centipedes with yellow-orange legs. They could be anywhere between 10 - 20 cm long and can move very fast when disturbed. A bite from a mukade can cause serious swelling and considerable pain, and if bitten, it is advisable to seek medical attention. Locals kill mukade on sight. Folklore suggests burning it or it will return from the dead to take revenge but a simple squash would suffice. Be watchful for them after heavy rain and especially around rainy season when they seek shelter inside.

SUZUMEBACHI HORNETS (大雀蜂) are the world's largest hornets and can be very aggressive if they detect a threat to their hive or food sources. They have a rather nasty sting much more toxic than a standard bee or wasp. General advice to prevent the unlikely interest of hornets in the mountains is to avoid strong perfumes, avoid wearing black and keep to the mountain trails. It is a common belief among farmers that the strength of the following typhoon season can be judged by the height of the hornets' nests in the trees. Low nests mean the storms will be severe and high that they will be mild.

JAPANESE GROUND BEETLES (マイマイカブリ) are common small black beetles with a long snout they use to eat snails with. When threatened they spray an acid mixture into the air which if it reaches your eyes will be very painful. Handle these with caution.

SNAKES

There are a variety of common snakes on Yakushima like the Japanese rat snake and the Oriental Odd-tooth but there are two that anyone venturing into the forest need to know about:

MAMUSHI (ニホンマムシ) or PIT VIPER has a dark colour and, like most vipers, has a distinctive triangular shaped head. Their bite is poisonous and very serious especially in the very young and old. Incidences of attacks are rare but they do happen: An elderly neighbour was killed by a mamushi while tending his field in Anbo and Kashima-san (my old boss) was temporarily paralysed in one side of his body after being bitten on the finger.

YAMAKAGASHI (ヤマカガシ) or TIGER KEELBACK has an irregular brown pattern with some reddish smudges and black stripes. These are often lurking around streams and rivers and as long as you walk slowly and firmly you have little chance of catching it basking in the sun within biting distance. It is poisonous however and its bite can be very serious. Its fangs are located at the back of its mouth which thankfully makes biting a large object like you and me a much more difficult prospect.

BIRDS

More than 167 bird species live on Yakushima. This includes endemic species like the Yakushima varied tit, distinctively smaller than the mainland tit, and the Yakushima Narcissus Flycatcher, lighter in colour than its mainland equivalent and with a distinctive yellow chest. There are other threatened species such as the Japanese Wood Pigeon, Izu Leaf-warbler, and the Izu Thrush which is easy to spot with its distinctive colouring - dark plumage, yellow eye rings and bill, brown wings, and a red chest. The Ryukyu Robin is considered so important that it has even been declared a Japanese Natural Monument.

SEA CREATURES

The Kuroshio Current (黒潮) splits south of Yakushima and flows both sides of the island wrapping it in all year round warm seas. The average sea temperature is between 20 and 30°C (68 – 86°F) and to illustrate how warm this is, as a fisherman on a flying fish trawler in chilly weather, I used to throw a bucket over the side and warm my cold hands in the water. This warmth allows a huge variety of fish to inhabit the waters around the island - there are thought to be at least 580 different species of fish.

There are also over 100 different species of coral that surround the island. They are a mixture of both temperate and tropical but, like much of the coral worldwide, are under threat due to 'coral bleaching'. This is the absence of an essential plant plankton called *Kacchuso* (zooxanthella) causing the coral to whiten and die. Of the many creatures inhabiting the sea around Yakushima, there are two species which are synonymous with the island:

TURTLES

LOGGERHEAD TURTLES (アカウミガメ) & **GREEN TURTLES** (アオウミガメ) are frequent visitors to Yakushima from May to July and many of them were born on the island's beaches. There are several official turtle nesting sites on the western side of the island where most of the turtles arrive but any one of the beaches around the coast can receive the turtles.

In the Nagata area there are three sandy beaches in a row. Maehama, in front of Nagata village, Inakahama, the longest stretch of sandy beach on the island (800 m), and Yotsusehama further north. The astonishing fact is that between them, these three beaches make up 40% of all loggerhead nesting in Japan. And because of this they are now protected as a 'Wetland of International Importance' under the Ramsar Convention.

Every year about 500 loggerhead turtles lay their eggs here. Female turtles start arriving between May and July to crawl up the beach, dig a hole with their back flippers and deposit 80-130 perfectly rounded eggs. Then 45-70 days later the eggs hatch and baby turtles scuttle down the beach to the sea. It is believed, though, that only 1 in 5,000 of these baby turtles actually reach maturity and will return one day to the island.

FLYING FISH

In May 2008, an NHK Japanese television crew filmed a flying fish off the coast of Yakushima which instantly made world news. It flew for 45 seconds and is thought to be one of the longest recorded flights by any flying fish (the previous record being 42 seconds in the 1920s).

Flying fish, known as *Tobiuo* (飛び魚), are able to fly because they have developed enlarged pectoral fins. They swim towards the surface of the water at great speed, leap out at a shallow angle and then, like an aeroplane, accelerate to take-off speed with their lateral fins spread wide and their tails beating the water. They then glide until there is no more lift and slide back into the water like Olympic divers.

It is thought that flying fish fly mainly to escape from predators, particularly Dolphin fish or Shira (シイラ) and it is very common for Dolphin fish to be caught in fishing nets alongside them. When Dolphin fish are caught they regurgitate the contents of their stomachs and these are usually the rotting carcasses of flying fish.

THE PEOPLE

People have been living on Yakushima since around 2000-1000 BC when it was known as the barbarous Yaku region. Its inhabitants were the Jomon people (縄文人) known for their distinctive rope-patterned pottery. In more recent times, the name 'Yakushima' crops up here and there in Japanese history linked to random events like the visiting of a Chinese envoy in the 8th Century and the landing of an Italian missionary named Sidocchi in the 18th Century, both of which suggest a sizable population. The current population is around 14,000 but as in the region of 315,000 tourists visit every year, it often feels much greater.

LOCAL FOLK STORIES

The following are a collection of local stories and legends involving creatures that were believed to influence life on Yakushima. They form part of the distinctive culture of Yakushima and were relayed to me by local people many of whom firmly believed in what they were telling. The grandfather of one of my neighbours, for example, swore that he had seen a Garappa in the local river and gave detailed descriptions about what it looked like and how it moved. Younger generations are not quite so convinced but they still know the stories all the same.

YAMA-NO-ONSUKE

One autumn, a hunter named Sasaki went to set a monkey trap with his brother between Nanako dake and Eboshi dake near Yudomari. It was getting dark so they decided to stay in Arake-no-miso, a shelter in the rocks.

After dinner, his brother went to sleep, but Sasaki stayed up and was enjoying the warmth of the fire. Suddenly, out of the forest he heard a scream: 'O-iiiiiii!' He immediately left the fire and looked around to see who was there. There was no one. But just as he began to return, he heard it again. This time instinctively he replied with the same shrill 'O-iiiiiii!' And waited for an answer. No one replied. But his shout had woken his brother who went very pale and told him to stop right away. Refusing to divulge why, he told his brother never to answer any call in the mountains. Sasaki was curious so he repeatedly asked his brother why until his brother eventually whispered in the quietest voice he could: 'Because YAMA-NO-ONSUKE will come'.

The voice suddenly came again but this time it sounded much louder and clearer. Sasaki jumped and was so surprised to hear it at such a close distance that, despite what his brother had told him, he instinctively replied. He regretted this immediately when the voice then screamed behind him. Both brothers scrambled together and looked out into the darkness. Silence. Sasaki picked up a stick, held it out to the dark and waited. The sound came again even closer. He desperately threw a piece of burning firewood to where he thought the voice was but could see nothing. Then both brothers backed their way into the cave and stood guard.

What followed was a sleepless night of scraping noises coming from the rock above their heads, and the sounds of trees falling and rocks tumbling. As much as they wanted to return home, they had to stay another night to tend the monkey trap but that night was even worse. Even shooting their gun in the air did not stop the noises in the darkness.

Their ordeal finally ended when they moved 1 km further down the mountain to Momijigadao for their third night and here all strange events ceased.

THE GODS OF MOCHOMU MOUNTAIN

One day an old man from Onoaida took his grandson to pick firewood in Miyakata, a mountain at the foot of Mochomu dake. While the old man and the boy were searching the undergrowth for sticks and fallen branches, a warm wind began to blow and the grass swayed strongly back and forth. The sound of a flute then followed and they could see the light of lanterns at the forest edge.

The old man had experienced this before and knew it to be a sign that the gods were passing. In October every year (October was known as 'no god month' [神無月] in the old Japanese calendar) all the gods in Yakushima went from Mochomu to a mountain called Wariishi dake. Fearing for the safety of his grandson, he instructed him to quickly lower his head while they passed.

But the grandson was curious like all little boys his age and he raised his head just in time to see something moving smoothly above the grass. He caught a glimpse of a creature with a red face, a white beard and white clothes disappearing towards Mochomu Mountain and at that instant became profoundly and permanently deaf.

THE VANISHING DEER ANTLERS

One clear autumn evening a local man named Sasaki, who was staying at the mountain shelter of Detaro iwaya, wandered off to hunt deer. He sat down on a Yakusugi stump and blew three times on his deer whistle to attract deer. He waited for a return call to signal a deer coming into his trap but instead he heard whispering. He jumped up and searched around but no one appeared to be there. He returned to the stump, blew the whistle again but the same thing happened. He moved closer to the sound and as he did, he saw a round black object twice the size of a human head.

Little creatures were coming out of the black ball and when he looked closer, they turned out to be long-legged frogs. He picked up a branch, hit the black object and hundreds of frogs dispersed in all directions. Underneath where the frogs had been, he noticed an antler. He picked it up but it was slimy so he washed it in a nearby stream. It immediately became brittle and snapped.

He then clearly understood why he had seen so few fallen antlers on his mountain trips - frogs eat the antlers – dissolving it with their mucous. He relayed this story to his disbelieving friends back in the village but to no avail, until a year later his friend saw the same spectacle and knowledge of the frogs in Hana-no-ego became widespread.

YAMAHIME (山姫)

One fine day, a farmer named Nagoe, went to Jigokudani behind Miyanoura dake to cut and collect bamboo trees. When he cut into the first bamboo, it began to pour with rain so he stopped, wiped the water off his face and tightened the straw shawl that kept the rain off. He heard a noise in the forest ahead and looked up. There, just inside the clearing, stood a beautiful woman in a colourful kimono. Before he could call out, he was dazzled by a blinding light and was pushed backwards so forcibly that he landed flat on his back. It started raining harder and harder and slowly he looked up from the ground. The woman was coming towards him.

He panicked, flung himself prostrate on the forest floor and begged for forgiveness promising he would never come here again. When he looked up again, she had stopped and was smiling at him. He prostrated himself again and recited prayers until he was so hoarse he could speak no more. Eventually the rain stopped. And when he gathered the courage to look up again she was gone. So he left all of the bamboo where it was and ran straight home, where he promptly fell ill and was bed ridden for a week.

This was Yamahime, the beautiful mountain princess. Legend says that when seen, she is so utterly beautiful that it is impossible to leave her gaze. Her hair is flowing and glistening, her skin pale as the moonlight and she is dressed in an immaculate red kimono. She smiles at her victims and if the smile is returned, she steals their life in an instant.

GARAPPA (ガラッパ)

An old man once went to Anbo River to wash his horse but the horse refused to get into the water. Annoyed at this, he tugged the horse by its reigns and forced it to bathe in the cool waters. Once the horse was clean the man returned home but he was quickly overcome by illness and was bed-ridden. He was told that this was the result of a curse by a Garappa.

A few days before a forest worker from Kosugidani, a village high in the mountains, had committed suicide and the rain had washed his dead body down to the river mouth. The Garappa, the water gods of Yakushima, had been holding a meeting about what to do with the corpse, when the man had disturbed and angered them. On hearing this, the old man returned to the same place at the riverside and apologised to where he thought the Garappa might be. His apology worked and he promptly recovered.

TENGU (天狗)

In October every year all the gods of Yakushima go to Izumo in Shimane Prefecture in the Chugoku region of mainland Japan. Without the gods to keep order in the mountains, all manner of lesser creatures descend out of the forest to celebrate. One of these is the Tengu, supernatural creatures with obscenely long noses or beaks, and they can be heard beating their drums on the mountain side throughout October. They gradually increase in volume during the night with the rhythm much faster towards sunrise until quiet descends on the forest at daybreak.

When walking in the mountains it is a common sight to see pine trees with branches crowded unnaturally together. This is because the first day of every month Tengu descend to the coast to retrieve water and on the way they rest on the branches. It is commonly known that anyone who cuts down these pine trees will be cursed forever by a Tengu. People are therefore reluctant to even go near these trees. If however one must be cut down, the night before an axe is put beside it and left until morning. If it is still in place the following day, the tree can be cut down. If the axe has fallen to the ground, the tree cannot be touched for fear of bringing the wrath of the Tengu.

THE WEATHER

The climate of Yakushima varies very much depending on altitude. Around the coast it is considered to be sub-tropical, although it gets distinctly chilly in winter. As you rise up the Mae dake (the frontal range) mountains around the coast it changes to warm temperate and then as you reach the central band of mountains in the centre of the island, it changes to cool-temperate. From here upwards to the summits, it is sub-Alpine.

So while the weather is usually mild around the coast, the inner mountains have a climate much more resembling Hokkaido in northern Japan. The average temperatures lie somewhere around 20°C (68°F) around the coast and 15°C (59°F) inland around Kosugidani, although the heat can be almost unbearable in summer and thick snow falls on the high mountains every winter as it reaches well below zero.

There are however variations on the above depending on how high you are on the mountains. The general rule is

	Av Temp	Max Temp	Min Temp
Jan	12.3	15.3	9
Feb	14.4	17.1	11.5
March	14.5	17.5	11.6
April	20.2	23.7	17.1
May	22.8	25.6	20.2
June	24.3	27.3	21.6
July	27	30.8	23.6
Aug	28	32.2	24.2
Sept	26.4	29.6	23.6
Oct	23.3	26	20.6
Nov	18.7	21.6	15.6
Dec	15	17.7	12.2

Temperatures (°C) in Yakushima

that for every 100 m you climb the temperature decreases by 0.6ºC. This means that you should allow for the following temperature changes in the mountains:

- At Shiratani Unsuikyo (825 m) it is 5ºC below the average.
- At Jomon Sugi (1300 m) it is 7.8ºC below.
- At Takatsuka Hut (1330 m) it is 8ºC below.
- At Yodogawa Hut (1380 m) it is 8.3ºC below.
- At Shintakatsuka Hut (1460 m) it is 8.8ºC below.
- At Shikanosawa Hut (1550 m) it is 9.3ºC below.
- At Ishizuka Hut (1600 m) it is 9.6ºC below.
- At the summit of Mt.Miyanoura (1936 m) it is 11.6ºC below.

Most people have heard about the legendary rainfall. The often quoted 35 days a month rain was actually taken from a popular novel published in the 1950s named 'Floating cloud' or 'Ukigumo' (浮雲) by Fumiko Hayashi (林芙美子), who once lived in Anbo in Yakushima and in which key scenes take place in the book.

The apparently high annual rainfall figure of 4,000 mm on the coast is deceptive. It does indeed rain but not as much as you might think with the 35 days thing. Half an hour of rain, a ray of sun, low clouds, a spot of rain again, cloud, and then boom, clear skies out of nowhere. The average visitor is usually far more confused about the weather than wet and soggy. Having said that though, when in the high mountains, there is much less confusion.

The average rainfall reaches up to 10,000 mm per year up here and the summits are often covered in dense cloud or mist. Unless the sky is clear of cloud expect the worst. There are two very notable additions to the general climate of Yakushima: Rainy season and typhoon season. Both have the ability to change travel plans in an instant.

RAINY SEASON (May - July) appears suddenly in early summer and levels of over 80% humidity can make hiding from the rain indoors quite uncomfortable and sticky. The general pattern is that it rains very hard most of the day but by early evening the skies clear and you ponder about all the things you could have done if the day had been like that from the start.

TYPHOON SEASON (July - Sept) can shut down the island for several days depending on the location and size of the storm. Well before the storm arrives the waves change shape and height and there is a distinctive feel to a pre-typhoon wave which is highly effective at inducing nausea.

When the typhoon gets closer the transport links shut down one by one. The fishing boats cannot leave port with wave heights over three metres and the jet foils usually stop operations any higher. The ferry can last a little longer but that too stops as the waves increase. The last to leave is the plane which gets busy with all the extra passengers from the boats. If you missed that, you would have to wait it out and join the rest of the island in boarding up, tying everything down and listening for bulletins over the loud speakers.

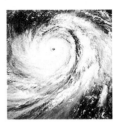

Typhoons invariably change direction and head on to terrorize China or into the Pacific. Occasionally however they hit full on with explosive force.

TYPHOON 17

Many years on and there has yet to be anything quite like Typhoon-Nabi (No.17 in the Japanese system). This was a category 5 Super Typhoon that formed on Aug 29th 2005 east of Saipan. It was of a similar strength to Hurricane Katrina which at the same time was devastating the southern States of the USA. It hit Yakushima in the early hours of Sept 6th and went on the following day to damage 10,000 homes, cause 168 landslides, and led to 143 injuries and 21 deaths on mainland Japan. Typhoon No.17 was travelling at a speed of 15 kph and because of this its full force lingered for two whole days, the winds reaching 160 kph and the waves a massive 9 m.

Our rented home was a sprawling wooden country house which was so old, it was on the verge of being swallowed by the forest. The wind pounded the north side of the house the whole day of Sept 5th, so we spent the night at the other end of the house in the annex room that jutted out into the garden.

In the early hours, the howling wind and the banging suddenly dropped. It was like flipping the off-switch. Insects were chirping, there were stars in the sky. Once the eye of the storm had passed over however, it all kicked off again but the direction of the gusts was now directly slamming into the sliding glass panels that lined three sides of the room.

We all feared the worse, dived under our bedding and hoped to last the night. In the end we did and by sunrise the house was still intact (-ish) and the winds calming. We ventured out to count our losses shortly after (one car, one roof and one cat) and ponder the raw power of nature.

WHEN TO GO

One of the most common questions we get at yakumonkey.com is when the best time to visit Yakushima is. You can in fact visit at any time of the year and still enjoy some of the magic that the island holds but here is a yearly breakdown on what to expect.

JANUARY

Off-season. Snow in the mountains and usually the coldest month of the year. No mountain buses running and mountain roads may close with heavy snowfall. Hiking not recommended for beginners.

FEBRUARY

Off-season. Still snow in the mountains and no mountain buses. At the end of the month a short rainy period called 'kinome nagashi' usually begins. Hiking not recommended for beginners.

MARCH

The 'kinome nagashi' rainy period usually lasts until mid-March. Still some snow on the higher mountains. Mountain buses begin running again. Spring school holiday at the end of March brings the first round of tourists and is usually busy. Still cold in the mountains.

APRIL

The Spring school holiday at the beginning of April means more visitors. Cherry blossoms bloom and are best seen from Taikoiwa Rock (See S1 in the Trails section). The forest is at its greenest. The end of the month brings 'Golden Week', a national holiday, and is the first peak-season of the year. Ideal to visit between the 2 holidays.

MAY

'Golden Week' holiday continues at the beginning of May and will be busy. Shakunage or rhododendron blossoms in the mountains throughout the month especially along Y1 trail. The forest is at its greenest. Yakumonkey baby season at the end of May.

JUNE

Rainy season begins. Waterfalls are at their strongest. Less hikers in the mountains. Yakumonkey baby season continues. Fireflies appear and can be seen in Yakushima Comprehensive Nature Park after dark.

JULY

Rainy season continues until mid-July and there are less tourists. Turtle egg laying season begins. Weather becomes hotter. School summer holidays begin at the end of the month which starts high season. Typhoon season also starts.

AUGUST

High season. Very hot. Turtle egg laying continues and the release of baby turtles begins. 'Obon' national holiday in mid August is the busiest time of the year. Typhoon season continues. The end of August is quieter with less tourists and is better for hiking.

SEPTEMBER

Early September is usually quiet and a good time to visit for this. Still hot and Typhoon season. 'Silver week' is another national holiday in mid to late September and is the last busy period of the year.

OCTOBER

Less rain and cooler temperatures. Ideal for hiking. Autumn leaves on the trails especially along Y1 Trail. Few tourists apart from weekends and consecutive holidays.

NOVEMBER

Less rain. Ideal for hiking. Autumn leaves on the Y1 Trail. Few tourists apart from weekends and consecutive holidays.

DECEMBER

Off-season and therefore quiet. Mountain buses stop running. Lower temperatures. Less daylight hours. Businesses close at New Year holidays. Occasional snow in the higher mountains.

THE BUSIEST TIMES FOR HIKING
- Golden Week - late April to mid May
- Obon Holiday - mid August
- Silver Week - mid September to late September
- National holidays

QUIETER TIMES FOR HIKING
- Between the School Spring holiday and Golden Week - mid April
- Late August to Early September (before Silver Week)
- November and December (apart from National holidays)

3 GETTING THERE & BACK

BY AIR

Japan Air Commuter (日本エアコミューター), a division of JAL, operates daily flights to Yakushima from three major Japanese cities: Kagoshima (in the South of Kyushu), Fukuoka (in the North of Kyushu) and Osaka (the second largest city in Japan). As the timetables of these planes are subject to change, I have not included them in this guide. You can find the latest timetables and more information about each flight at yakumonkey.com and www.jal.co.jp/en.

KAGOSHIMA (鹿児島)

JAL operates a JAC propeller plane 5 times a day from Kagoshima airport and the flight takes around 35 mins to cover 102 miles. The route south flies over Sakurajima volcano and offers wonderful views if you get good weather.

Prices and timetables vary according to the season and how far in advance you book. As a rough guide, one way should be approx. ¥14,000 ~ and return ¥26,000 ~. You can book and find current timetables in English at www.jal.co.jp/en.

FUKUOKA (福岡)

JAL operate a DHC8-Q400 74 seater between Fukuoka and Yakushima once a day. The flight takes around 65 minutes.

Price and timetables vary according to the season and how far in advance you book. As a rough guide, one way should be approx. ¥25,000 ~ and return ¥46,000 ~. You can book and find current timetables in English at www.jal.co.jp/en.

OSAKA (大阪)

There is 1 daily direct flight in a 74 seater DHC8-Q400 to/from Osaka Itami airport. The distance travelled is over 402 miles and takes around 90 minutes.

Price varies according to the season and how far in advance you book. As a rough guide, one way should be approx. ¥34,000 ~ and return ¥62,000 ~. Current timetables can be found at www.jal.co.jp/en.

BY SEA

GET TO KAGOSHIMA PORT (鹿児島港)

If you come via Kagoshima airport and catch a ferry or jetfoil please note that the airport is over 50 mins by road north of the port. Make sure you factor this in when choosing your travel connections.

There is a shuttle bus, called the Airport Limousine Bus (空港リムジンバス), which for ¥1,200 takes you to Kagoshima Main port (鹿児島本港). The bus for Kagoshima City is line No.2 and colour coded in red. Note that not all buses go as far as the port. Only bus times in bold go on to the Port Terminal (高速船ターミナル), the others stop in the city centre.

If you arrive at Kagoshima Chuo Train Station (鹿児島中央駅) a taxi takes 15 min, the Rosen bus (路線バス) takes 20 min and the 'Dolphin 150' shuttle bus (ドルフィン150) takes 16 min to the Dolphin port which is only a short walk to the South Wharf Port terminals.

Facing Sakurajima, the Tane-Yaku Jetfoil Terminal is the triangular building to the right. Go further into the port area and the Mishima and Toshima Terminals are on the left and right respectively. The Minami-futo Wharf Traveller's Terminal (南埠頭旅客ターミナル) is at the end and Ferry Yakushima 2 leaves to the right of this. You should see the large signs in English.

TANE-YAKU JET FOIL (ジェットフォイル トッピー ロケット)

If you want to go by sea, this is the fastest way. There are 7 round-trip journeys to/from Yakushima by Jetfoil every day. They leave from Tane-Yaku Jetfoil Port (種子・屋久高速船旅客ターミナル) near the

center of Kagoshima, next to the Dolphin Port entertainment area. It is easy to find and, depending on your luggage, is perfectly walkable from the center of the city. While there is only one Jetfoil port in Kagoshima, there are actually 2 in Yakushima. Some jetfoils go via Miyanoura (宮之浦) in the North of Yakushima and some of them go via

Anbo (安房) in the East. If there are no alphabetized words, look for these characters on the timetable to be sure of your destination.

Many of the jetfoil journeys make a stop on the way either at Tanegashima (種子島), the neighbouring island to Yakushima, or Ibusuki (指宿), in Kagoshima Prefecture. On the timetable it might say '種経由' (literally 'via Tane') which means 'via Tanegashima' and in a similar way '指経由' means 'via Ibusuki'. It does not matter which route you take, only that the destination is Yakushima (屋久島) and either Anbo (安房) or Miyanoura (宮之浦). Look for these charac-

ters and you will start to understand the timetable a little. You can find the most up-to-date timetable at the jetfoil website at www.tykousoku.jp/fare_time.

Once on board, you get to choose whether to sit on the upper or lower floor but once you sit, you put your seatbelt on and you stay put. You cannot wander around as you would on a ferry. There is a drink machine and toilets but an attendant who will tell you off if you do decide to stretch your legs. The best thing about the jetfoil is that it is fast. If time is an issue, it is a good choice.

Prices can depend on the season but it should be approx. ¥8,300 ~ one way and ¥15,000 ~ return. More information can be found at yakumonkey.com (in English) and the official website - tykousoku.jp (in Japanese).

NOTE: If you want to reserve a boat and you are oversees/ do not speak Japanese, your accommodation may help. Shikinoyado Onoaida and Morinokokage for example provide this service for their guests (see accommodation section for more details). There is also a local Japanese travel agency (Yakushima travel) which has a very convenient booking service for jetfoil tickets. They will reserve the tickets for you in advance for a ¥500 fee. They have an English page here: www.yakushimatravel.com/ticket-english.html

If there is bad weather and the wave height rises above 3 m both jet foils may be cancelled. You can get a refund if you have bought your ticket already. If they are cancelled, try the ferry as it often continues to run or try the plane which rarely cancels due to the weather.

FERRY YAKUSHIMA 2 (フェリー屋久島2)

There is one dedicated passenger ferry a day from Kagoshima. It arrives at lunchtime in Yakushima and leaves an hour later to arrive back in Kagoshima in the early evening. The ferry leaves from Kagoshima at Minami-futo Wharf Traveller's Terminal (南埠頭旅客ターミナル) which is very conveniently located close to the center of Kagoshima and a short distance further on from the Jetfoil Port.

The ferry is large and comfortable and provides a carpeted area to lie down on to your left as you climb aboard and there are chairs to lounge in if you go upstairs. If you have the time, it is a scenic way to arrive as you can appreciate the size and shape of the island as it draws closer in the distance.

The price varies according to season but should be approx. ¥4,900 ~ one way and ¥8,900 ~ return. You cannot get a ticket online but it is possible to buy a ticket on any LOPPI ticket machine in Lawson convenience stores in Japan (if you can read Japanese). Otherwise you will need to turn up and buy a ticket from either the automatic machine inside or from the ticket booths. You first need to fill in a short form which is on

the counter near the ticket booth. All you need to do is write your name on the form and hand it to the person in the ticket booth. Up to date prices and timetables can be found at yakumonkey.com and the official website: http://ferryyakusima2.com.

FERRY HIBISCUS (フェリーはいびすかす)

Ferry Hibiscus is a cargo ferry which also takes passengers, which means that luxury is not something that you should expect if you travel aboard. It leaves in the early evening and then docks at Tanegashima for the night. You then have to sleep in a shared carpeted area and eat from the instant noodle dispensing machine. It does not set off again until sunrise and then docks in Yakushima in the early morning. The homeward bound trip is slightly less of an ordeal. It leaves Yakushima first thing in the morning, stops only for an hour in Tanegashima and gets to Kagoshima shortly after lunch.

The fare to Yakushima should be approx. ¥3,300 ~ one way and ¥6,600 ~ return. Up to date prices and timetables can be found at yakumonkey.com and the official website: www.yakushimaferry.com

NOTE: This ferry operates from a different port in Kagoshima called Taniyama Port (谷山港). You can get there by bus, taxi or train, depending where you start from. As there is only 1 ferry bus from the city center, I have given you more options so that you can get to the port on time.

Here are the options:

GET TO TANIYAMA PORT (谷山港)

1. FROM KAGOSHIMA AIRPORT (鹿児島空港)

1. Take the Airport limousine bus from Kagoshima Airport to Kagoshima City Center (鹿児島市内) which costs ¥1,200 and takes 50 min. Get off at Kagoshima Chuo Train Station (鹿児島中央駅) and follow the instructions below for train or bus, or get off at Tenmonkan (天文館) in the city center and follow the instructions for the bus.

2. Take the direct bus from Kagoshima Airport to Taniyama (谷山) which takes 55 min and leaves every half an hour. You need to get off at Oroshihonmachi Chuo (卸本町中央). It costs ¥1,450 one way. You are now in Taniyama but you need to catch a taxi to the actual port. Take a taxi to Taniyama Port (谷山港) which takes 5 min and costs ~ ¥1,500. There should be a taxi rank nearby.

2. FROM KAGOSHIMA CHUO TRAIN STATION (鹿児島中央駅)

1. A taxi from Kagoshima Chuo Train Station to Taniyama Port costs about ¥4,330 and will take about 36 min to cover the 13.4 km distance.

2. Take the train from Kagoshima Chuo Train Station to Sakanoue Station (坂之上駅) on the JR Ibusuki-Makurazaki line (JR指宿枕崎線). The journey takes 20 min and costs ¥280. From Sakanoue Station take a taxi to Taniyama Port (谷山港) which takes 15 min and costs ¥2,000.

3. Take the Ferry bus which comes from the city center as detailed below. It arrives at 15.48 and costs around ¥380.

3. FROM KAGOSHIMA CITY CENTER (鹿児島市内)

1. The Ferry bus from Kagoshima City center leaves Kinseicho (金生町発) at 15.40. Walk towards Sakurajima from Tenmonkan and the bus stop is near the corner of the main intersection where the tram turns left. The tram stop nearby is Izurodori Station (いづろ通駅). The Taniyama Port bus stop is at the Yamagataya Bus Center (山形屋バスセンター) between Kagoshima Bank and Mizuho Bank and if you follow the tram line around to the left, it is on the other side of the road. The bus then goes on to Kagoshima Chuo Train Station (鹿児島中央駅) at 15.48 and then arrives at Taniyama Port at 16.34. The journey costs only around ¥380.

If you come the opposite way, the bus leaves Taniyama Port at 15.16 and arrives at Kagoshima Chuo Train Station at 16.02 and then Kinseicho at 16.09.

4 MOVING AROUND

The best way of moving around Yakushima depends on many variables: the duration of your stay, the time of year, your destinations, your inclinations etc. Most people tend to hire a car but the new day 'free pass' may make the bus a more viable option. Scooters and motorbikes can be rented, or mountain bikes if you do not mind the ups and downs. Walking is of course the mode of transport of the mountains and it is quite feasible to walk from the port in Miyanoura straight to the Shiratani Hut and across the island without the need of anything save for two, soon to be very weary, legs.

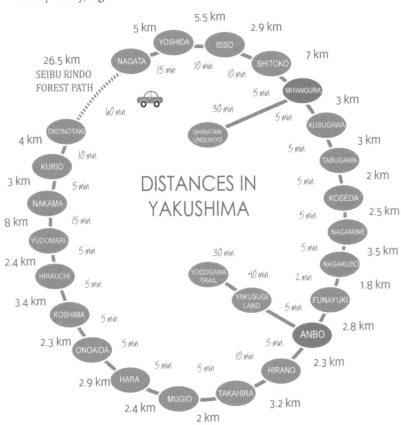

RENT A CAR

The most convenient way to travel in Yakushima is by rental car and there are many car hire outlets on the island competing with each other. Most of the companies are near the airport in Koseda and the ports in Miyanoura and Anbo. With so much competition, it is worth shopping around for the best deal at the time you want to visit. Also check with your accommodation as they sometimes have car hire services.

The prices range between ¥4,000 - ¥6,000 for 1 day and ¥8,000 - ¥10,000 for 2 days for the smallest car; then for a medium car (1500 cc), 1 day is ¥6,000 to ¥8,000 and 2 days ¥12,000 and ¥15,000; a more powerful car (2000 cc) rises to ¥13,000 for 1 day and ¥22,000 for 2 days; and should you require a people wagon for 6-7 people, 1 day's rental is ¥13,000 to ¥16,000. The minimum rental period is 6 hours and then it rises to 9, 12, 24, 36 and 48 hours. If you require a car for longer than 48 hours, it must be by the day not the hour. So the minimum after 48 hours is 72 hours. Should you then be late in returning the car, any extra time is by the hour.

LOCAL OPTIONS

• Check with your accommodation first as many now offer car rental packages which might be good value.
• **SUZUKI RENTALEASE** (70 cars) (スズキレンタリース) in Miyanoura and **JNET RENTACAR** (Jネットレンタカー) in Anbo. We have known this local company for 10 years and they have consistently been approachable and professional. They have always rented to foreigners and have an English speaker. Hours: 08.30 – 19.00. Web 1: http://www.suzuki-rentalease.co.jp (Japanese) Web 2: www.j-netrentacar.co.jp/kagoshima/yakushima (Japanese). You can email them in English at nakashima@po3.synapse.ne.jp. TEL 42-1772.
• **CAMGO** (2 cars) have 2 small camping cars to rent so you could combine paying for accommodation and transport. They sleep 2 comfortably and are equipped with bedding, a table and chairs and cooking equipment. The benefit of renting a camping car is that you can park it overnight at the trail entrances or by the sea and take advantage of the toilet facilities which are usually nearby. Web: http://camgo-yakushima.sakuraweb.com/english/index.html (English website). Book direct in English.
• **YAKUSHIMA SOUTH VILLAGE** (屋久島サウスビレッジ) rents out its fleet of 5 Suzuki cars by the hour/day. Tel: 47-3751 Web: yakushima-yh.net (English website) Email: yakushimasouth@gmail.com

NATIONAL CHAINS

- **TOYOTA RENTALEASE** (トヨタレンタリース) (96 cars) Tel: 42-2000 Web: https://rent.toyota.co.jp/eng/index.aspx (English website)
- **RENTAL CAR GROUP** Web: http://japan.rentalcargroup.com/yakushima_airport.htm (English website)
- **EUROPCAR** Tel: 43-5700 Web: www.europcar.com/location/japan/kumage-gum/yakushima-airport (English website)
- **NIPPON RENTACAR** (20 cars) (ニッポンレンタカー) Tel: 49-4189 Web: www.nrgroup-global.com/en/ (English website)
- **TIMES CAR RENTAL** (19 cars) (タイムズカーレンタル) Miyanoura: Tel: 43-5700 Web: www.timescar-rental.com (English website)
- **ORIX RENTACAR** (25 cars) (オリックスレンタカー) Tel: 42-2669 Web: car.orix.co.jp/rent/shop (English website)

INSURANCE & THE NOC

All companies include liability insurance and damage insurance in the basic contract charges that they quote you. If you have an accident or damage another car, insurance companies will pay up to the limit of liability. There is usually an excess amount that the rental user is required to pay and this is usually reduced with the Collision Damage Waiver (CDW) system. The industry standard is ¥50,000, although if you pay more, you can reduce it. This is pretty normal the world over so far.

What is not normal and what you need to get your head around when renting a car in Japan is the Non Operation Charge (NOC). This kicks in when there has been an incident and the rental car needs to be repaired and/or cleaned due to damage. As the car can no longer be used to rent to other customers, the rental company has the right to charge a fee independent of any insurance claims by way of compensation. And that fee is charged to the rental user. The industry standard is ¥20,000 if the car is still drivable and ¥50,000 if the car is not drivable. This means that should you be in an accident, through no fault of your own, and the car sustains damage, you will be liable for the NOC fee. No amount of shouting, screaming, pleading or general huffing and puffing will sway the rental company in this. It is a Japan-wide policy. When you sign the rental contract, you are agreeing to this.

This means that your liability as a rental user is that, in the event of an accident, you have to pay the excess of ¥50,000 and if another car was involved you may also pay their excess of ¥50,000 (Yes, you read that right), and on top of this the NOC fee of ¥50,000. So you could in theory have a bill of up to ¥150,000 for a minor collision. Of course, this does not happen very often but you need to be aware that such a system exists if only to prepare yourself for the worst!

DRIVING LICENCE

The one essential thing you need if you do not have a Japanese licence is an International Driving Licence. Without this you will not be allowed to rent. If your licence is from France, Belgium, Germany, Monaco, Slovenia, Switzerland and Taiwan you need to bring the licence and an official Japanese translation by the JAF (Japan Automobile Association) or by the embassy or consulate office in Japan.

DRIVING RULES

Drinking and driving in Japan is punished severely. If you drive while under the influence of alcohol and fail a breath test, you face up to 3 years in prison or a ¥500,000 fine. If you are a passenger in the car, you are deemed responsible and will be fined. If you run the bar where the driver was served the alcohol, you are also legally responsible and will be fined. So do not be surprised if you are refused alcohol on Yakushima if you are the driver of a vehicle parked outside. This is to prevent everyone involved from being punished.

When you come to an intersection, and you see a stop sign, you should completely stop the car before moving on. The driver is supposed to look left and right when the car is stopped. This rule is enforced and you may be fined if a police officer sees. Also if there is an accident, the driver who did not stop their car is apportioned full responsibility no matter what.

The roads, bar one or two mountain tracks, are sealed and well maintained and driving on Yakushima is relatively uncomplicated. There is essentially one continuous road around the island with only a hand-ful of traffic signals in the larger villages and anyone used to driving on the mainland will be pleasantly surprised. Some of the car parks are very small, as at Oko-no-taki Waterfall, for example, so be prepared to park in tight spots by the road side (watch out for unprotected drains running at the side of the road).

GO BY BUS

There are two main bus companies on Yakushima: the **YAKUSHIMA KOUTSU BUS** (屋久島交通バス) and the **MATSUBANDA BUS** (まつばんだ交通バス). Although sometimes their routes shadow each other, most of the time they service different parts of Yakushima. The larger of the two is Yakushima Kotsu Bus which is the main bus that services the whole coastal area and the two mountain roads. The Matsubanda bus is more connected to tourism and provides early morning and afternoon buses to Yakusugi museum for hikers con-necting to/from Arakawa Trail buses and also up to Shiratani Unsuikyo.

Each Yakushima Koutsu bus stop (the bus stop sign on the right) has a number on it which corresponds to the number on the bus timetable. In this case you can see 72 which means that it is the Kigensugi bus stop. The Matsubanda sign (the sign on the left) is not numbered here but uses the same stop numbers. This numbering system is useful as it means you do not have to remember unfamiliar names.

FREE PASS

The Yakushima Koutsu Bus has a bus pass called *FREE PASS* (フリー乗車券) whereby 1 day costs ¥2,000, 2 days cost ¥3,000, 3 days are ¥3,000 and 4-day passes are ¥4,000, all with children at half price. You can get on and off the bus as many times as you want during that period but it is only valid for the Yakushima Koutsu bus NOT the Matsubanda bus. You can also show your pass for a ¥100 discount at Yakusugi museum, Yakusugiland or Shiratani Unsuikyo. Please also note that this pass is not valid for the Arakawa Trekking Bus nor any tour buses.

Annoyingly you cannot just buy the pass on the bus – but you can however buy it at these places before you get on:

OUTSIDE OF YAKUSHIMA
- Kagoshima & Ibusuki Port (Jetfoil and Ferry Terminals)
- Ibusuki & Kirishima Iwasaki Hotel

ON YAKUSHIMA
Miyanoura area
- Miyanoura port (宮之浦港) No.20 bus stop
- Yakushima Kanko Centre (屋久島観光センター) No.21 bus stop
- Yakushima Youth Hostel (屋久島ユースホステル) No.21 bus stop
- Seaside Hotel Yakushima (シーサイドホテル屋久島) No.19 bus stop
- Yakushima Environmental Culture Village Center (屋久島環境文化村センター) No.20 bus stop
- Tourist Information Center (観光案内所) No.20 bus stop

Koseda area
- Yakushima Airport (屋久島空港) No.49 bus stop
- Tourist Information Center (観光案内所) No.49 bus stop

Anbo area
- Anbo Port (安房港) No.64 bus stop
- Anbo Eco Town Awaho (エコタウンあわほ) No.64 bus stop
- Anbo Tourist Information center (観光案内所) No.66 bus stop
- Mori-no-kirameki (森のきらめき) No.63 bus stop
- Outside Yakusugi Museum at the No.68 bus stop

Onoaida area
- JR Hotel Yakushima (ＪＲホテル屋久島) No.97 bus stop

- Yakushima Iwasaki Hotel (屋久島いわさきホテル) No.99 bus stop
Hirauchi area
- Yakushima South Village (屋久島サウスビレッジ) No.107 bus stop

TIMETABLES

For bus timetables, the most up-to-date will be on yakumonkey.com. They are notoriously late to be published and are usually revised during the year so I have learnt my lesson from previous editions of the book, and will not be including them here.

PRICES

If you cannot use the free pass, you pay directly on the bus. Some of the prices of common one-way journeys are as follows:

- Anbo port to Yakusugi museum = ¥230
- Anbo port to Y3 Yakusugiland = ¥740
- Anbo Port to Kigensugi (Y1 Yodogawa Trail) = ¥940
- Anbo port to Okonotaki = ¥1,320
- Anbo port to Nagata = ¥1,480
- Yakusugi Museum to A1 Arakawa Trail = ¥870
- Miyanoura port to S1 Shiratani Unsuikyo = ¥550
- Miyanoura port to Nagata = ¥900
- Miyanoura port to Anbo = ¥830
- Miyanoura port to Okonotaki = ¥1,870

ARAKAWA MOUNTAIN BUS

The entrance to the Arakawa Trail (A1) which is the main trail used to hike to Jomon Sugi has access restrictions to try and lessen the environmental impact of tourism on Yakushima. Basically you cannot just drive there anymore. You either need to take the special Arakawa bus, a pre-arranged taxi or be on a guided tour.

The Arakawa Mountain bus runs from the beginning of March to the end of November and starts outside Yakusugi museum in Anbo. Tickets should be bought before getting on the bus and can be bought in tourist information centers, convenience stores, climbing gear shops, souvenir shops, taxi companies, various accommodations and with guides. One way for an adult is ¥870 and a child ¥350. If you plan to return the same way, you need two one way tickets. Should you arrive with no ticket, do not panic, you can actually buy one at Yakusugi Museum Arakawa bus stop. Make sure you check the timetables beforehand as they change frequently. You can find the latest timetable at yakumonkey.com.

RENT A BICYCLE

Bicycles are fairly cheap and easy to rent and are a great way to experience the best of the island. There are plenty of ups and downs on the coastal road and as long as you prepare yourself that it will not all be hands-free gliding, it is a very enjoyable and rewarding activity. The only really taxing parts of the coastal road are the ascents on the Seibu Rindo Forest Path (西部林道) in the West of the island. Should you wish to circumnavigate the island in one go, it takes around 8-9 hours and is probably easier travelling clockwise.

Bike rental requires a deposit for the time you have rented the bike and costs usually around ¥1,200 a day for a mountain bike. Check with your accommodation or try the following:

Miyanoura area
- **YAKUSHIMA KANKO CENTER** (屋久島観光センター) has 6-gear bikes for ¥1,000 a day which you can return at Mori-No-Kirameki (see below). It also has 21-gear mountain bikes for ¥1,500 a day. Tel: 42-0091 Web: yksm.com

Anbo area
- **MORI-NO-KIRAMEKI** (森のきらめき) has 6-gear bikes for ¥1,000 a day. You can return your bike at Yakushima Kanko Center (see above) Tel: 49-7101 Web: morinokirameki.com
- **YOU SHOP NANGOKU** (南国) in Anbo has a range of bikes from ¥800 to ¥3,000 yen a day. They also have hourly rates available (¥200 an hour). Web: http://youshop-nangoku.jimdo.com (click on レンタルサイクル to see the bikes).

Hirauchi area
- **YAKUSHIMA SOUTH VILLAGE** has 5-gear bikes for ¥800 a day and 24-gear mountain bikes for ¥1,200 a day. Web: http://yakushimasouth.wix.com/south.

RENT A SCOOTER

Motorbikes or scooters can be rented at these places:
Miyanoura area

- **SUZUKI RENTALEASE** (スズキレンタリース) offers 50cc bikes for rent for 1 hour, 9 hours and 24+ hours. 24 hours rental costs ¥4,000 and each day after that is at ¥3,000. They are used to renting to non-Japanese and you can book directly with them in English by email and make your language simple and clear. Hours: 08.30 – 19.00. Web: www.suzuki-rentalease.co.jp/rentalbike. Email: nakashima@po3.synapse.ne.jp. Tel: 42-1772.

Anbo area

- **YOU SHOP NANGOKU** (南国) offers 50cc bikes for ~ ¥3,500 for 24 hours. The selection bikes is good but no English is spoken and I wonder how interested the owner is in foreign customers, as after so many years, he still offers nothing in English. Web: https://youshop-nangoku.jimdo.com Tel: 46-2705.

GO BY TAXI

Taxis are often invaluable when arriving and departing but hikers also often use taxis to take and collect them from the mountain trails in the early hours of the morning and late afternoon. Should you need one, get the help of your accommodation, go to the taxi offices or phone to reserve it.

If you want to take a taxi up to the beginning of the Arakawa trail (A1), each passenger has to buy a road usage ticket for ¥180 one way in addition to the fare.

There are three main taxi companies in Yakushima:

- **MATSUBANDA KOUTSU** (まつばんだ交通タクシー) has offices in Miyanoura and Anbo Tel: 43-5000/43-5555 (12 taxis).
- **YAKUSHIMA KOUTSU** (屋久島交通タクシー) is also in Miyanoura and Anbo Tel: 42-0611 (24 taxis)
- **ANBO TAXI** (安房タクシー) is only in Anbo Tel: 46-2311 (8 taxis).

5 PRACTICALITIES

POST OFFICE

There are two main post offices or yubinkyoku (郵便局) on Yakushima:
- **ANBO POST OFFICE** (安房郵便局) is on the Anbo Port turn-off, a short distance from Kagoshima Bank (鹿児島銀行).
- **MIYANOURA POST OFFICE** (宮之浦郵便局) is near Miyanoura Bridge in the village center. Turn towards the sea at the second turning after the bridge and it is on your right.

Both have ATM machines available (which will accept major credit cards). There are also smaller post offices, with limited facilities, in most of the other villages.

MONEY/BANKS

Cash is still the only form of currency readily accepted in Yakushima. Credit or debit cards are not widely accepted outside of the big hotels. **KAGOSHIMA BANK** (鹿児島銀行) and **MINAMI NIHON BANK** (南日本銀行) have branches in Miyanoura and Anbo. Kagoshima bank does now have facilities for currency exchange - you can change cash and travellers checks in major currencies there. Both banks also have ATM machines which accept major credit cards, however card compatibility can sometimes be an issue.

Post offices also have ATMs in Miyanoura, Anbo and Onoaida and will accept most major credit cards.

WI-FI

Wi-Fi is available at the following places:

Miyanoura area
- **KITCHEN & CAFE HITOMEKARI** (ヒトメクリ) on Route 77 near the hospital
- **YAKUSHIMA GALLERY REST CAFE** above Yakushima Kanko center (屋久島観光センター) near the port.
- **PANORAMA** (パノラマ) restaurant in the center of Miyanoura
- **RYUHOU** (龍鳳) restaurant close to the shrine in Miyanoura

Koseda area
- **YAKUSHIMA MESSENGER** (屋久島メッセンジャー) outdoor store and cafe on Route 77 south of the airport.
- **IL MARE** (イルマーレ) restaurant next to the airport

- **AIRPORT HOTEL** (屋久島エアポートホテル) next to the airport
- **HIBISCUS** (ハイビスカス) restaurant on Route 77 south of the airport

Anbo area
- **YORONZAKA** (よろん坂) cafe on Route 77 going up the hill south of Anbo
- **SANPOTEI** (散歩亭) pub on the south side of Anbo River near Manten Bridge
- **JIJI YA** (じいじ家) restaurant on the north side of Anbo River near Manten Bridge

Mugio area
- **VITA KITCHEN** (ヴィータキッチン) on the mountain side of Route 77

Hara area
- **NOMADO** (ノマドカフェ) café on Route 77 south of Hara (mountain side)
- **DOUBUCHI** (どうぶち) restaurant on Route 77 south of Hara (sea side)

GAS STATIONS

There are no gas stations on the western side of the island between Kurio and Nagata. Gas stations are generally open from 08.30 to 19.00 but many are closed on weekends. In the larger villages like Anbo, Miyanoura and near the airport, gas stations are usually open at weekends (incl. Sundays) but most open according to a rota so the exact gas station which opens is changeable. 'Self' gas station in Koseda (next to Some's) is usually open when others are not. It is of course best if possible to fill up before Sunday to avoid wasting time searching.

SUPERMARKETS/CONVENIENCE STORES

Miyanoura area
- **WAI WAI LAND** (わいわいランド) is opposite the hospital. Hours: 09.00 – 20.00 Tel: 42-2525.
- **A CO-OP** (Aコープ) is on the mountain road to Shiratani Unsui-kyo. Hours: 09.30 – 20.00 Tel: 42-3888.
- **LIFE CENTRE YAKUDEN** (ライフセンターヤクデン) 200 m past Yakushima Environmental Culture Village Centre on the main road heading towards Nagata. Hours: 09.00 – 22.00. Tel: 42-1501.
All the above sell a wide selection of food and many other things like clothes, DIY equipment and furniture. Life Centre Yakuden also sells

camping and fishing equipment.

• **AI SHOP IMAMURA** (アイショップいまむら) is a convenience store near the intersection to Shiratani Unsuikyo in Miyanoura. Hours: 08.00 - 23.00. Tel: 42-0315.

Koseda area

• **DRUGSTORE MORI** (ドラッグストアモリ) is a large drugstore which sells so much more than medicine. Hours: 09.00 – 22.00. Tel: 43-5505.

• **DRUG ELEVEN** (ドラッグイレブン) is very similar and is next door and it also has a very useful ¥100 section. Hours: 09.00 – 21.00. Tel: 49-4141.

• **SOME'S** (サムズ) hardware store sells a limited selection of food but mostly camping gear, fishing equipment, clothes and DIY. Hours: 09.00 – 21.00. Tel: 43-5963.

• **M MART** (エムマート) is on Route 77 in Koseda village Hours: 09.00- 20.00. Tel: 43-5265.

Anbo area

• **A CO-OP** (Aコープ) is within a building called 'Eco-Town Awaho' (エコタウンあわほ) with a handful of smaller stores. It is opposite the Toppy jet foil port and sells packed lunches and snacks as well as more general food. Hours: 09.00 – 20.00 (19.00 in winter). Tel: 49-7820.

• **TANAKA SEIKA** (田中青果・生花) is on Route 77 near the Green Hotel and is a general supermarket Hours: 08.30 - 20.00. Tel: 46-4567.

• **SHIBA** (しいば) is just before the mountain road to Yakusugiland and is renowned for its freshly baked bread and cakes Hours: 08.00 – 20.00. Tel: 46-2067.

Onoaida area

• **A CO-OP** (Aコープ) is also in Onoaida near the main intersection on the by-pass road. At the traffic signals turn towards Onoaida and the supermarket is on your right Hours: 09.00 – 20.00 (19.00 in winter). Tel: 47-2611.

• **AI SHOP ONOAIDA** (アイショップ) convenience store is on the by-pass at the north end of the village. Tel: 47-2140.

Kurio area

• **S MART** (Sマート) convenience store is in the centre of Kurio and sells a wide selection of food and drink. Tel: 48-2805.

Isso area

• **MARUICHI STORE** (まるいちストアー) is in the centre of Isso. Hours: 08.00 - 19.00. Tel: 44-2049.

BOOKSTORES

- **TOMARI SHOTEN** (泊書店) has a bookshop in Anbo as the road bends down to the river, after the police station. They sell books, magazines and maps. Hours: 09.00 – 19.00. Tel: 46-3111.
- **SHOSEN FLORA** (書泉フローラ) is on the main street in Miyanoura between the 2nd and 3rd traffic signals from the river. Tel: 42-0134.

TOURIST INFORMATION CENTER

There are Tourist Information Centers in the following places:
- Miyanoura, inside the Port Building. Tel: 42-1019.
- Koseda, near the entrance of the airport car park. Tel: 49-4010.
- Anbo, near Moss burger at the intersection before Anbo Bridge. Tel: 46-2333.

LAUNDRY

There are 24-hour automated laundrettes in various locations around the island. There is one next to SOME'S (サムズ) hardware store in Koseda, in Miyanoura behind Life Store Yakuden (ライフセンターヤクデン) and near A Co-op (Aコープ) supermarket, and in Anbo next to You Shop Nangoku (南国) on the main road. These have washing machines, driers and specialist equipment like shoe washer/driers.

GARBAGE

There are very few public litter bins on the island and you are expected to carry whatever you use until you can dispose of it at your accommodation or other appropriate place.

POLICE

The main police station, **YAKUSHIMA KEISATSUSHO** (屋久島警察署), is in Anbo, at the top of the hill on the main road leading down to the river. There are smaller stations in most of the villages. As with the rest of Japan, the emergency number to call for the police is 110.

HOSPITALS & CLINICS

There is one main hospital on the island:
- **YAKUSHIMA TOKUSHUKAI** (屋久島徳州会病院) Tel: 42-2200. It is on the main coastal road in Miyanoura, opposite Wai Wai Land (わいわいランド) supermarket.

There are also smaller but well-equipped clinics in other larger villages:

- **KOSEDA SHINRYOJO** (小瀬田診療所) Tel: 43-5100 in Koseda. Tuesdays only.
- **NAKAIIN** (仲医院) Tel: 46-2131 in Anbo.
- **ONOAIDA SHINRYOJO** (尾之間診療所) Tel: 47-3277 in Ono-aida.

The emergency number for an ambulance is 119.

COIN LOCKERS

Coin lockers to store your luggage are available at **YAKUSHIMA KANKO CENTRE** (屋久島観光センター) in Miyanoura Tel: 42-0091 and **MORI-NO-KIRAMEKI** (森のきらめき) in Anbo Tel: 49-7101 Web: morinokirameki.com
- Large (80 cm x 40 cm x 40 cm) costs ¥500 for 48 hours.
- Small (40 cm x 40 cm x 40 cm) costs ¥300 for 48 hours.

There are also facilities in **FURUSATOICHIBA** (ふるさと市場) in Miyanoura and Anbo Port.

BAGGAGE FORWARDING

YAKUSHIMA KANKO CENTRE (屋久島観光センター) and **FURUSATOICHIBA** (ふるさと市場) in Miyanoura, near the Port and **MORI-NO-KIRAMEKI** (森のきらめき) in Anbo, will also send your bags on to anywhere on the island. This could be very convenient if you are crossing the mountains and want to stay the other side of the island. The cost is normally ¥300 per item.

ACCOMMODATION BASICS

There is a wide variety of accommodation on Yakushima from top of the range hotels to basic mountain huts and to help you find the best place to stay, I have narrowed down the choices in the following sections. If you wish to stay in the FREE MOUNTAIN HUTS you will find more details of them in the hiking section.

Japanese accommodation names reveal what kind of accommodation is offered.
- HOTEL (ホテル): A modern hotel resembling those in the West.
- RYOKAN (旅館): A traditional inn, serving traditional food, with tatami rooms.
- PENSION (ペンション): A small modern guest house.
- MINSHUKU (民宿): A converted house, rooms are usually tatami mat and traditional.
- SUDOMARI MINSHUKU (素泊まり民宿): Similar to a minshuku but does not serve food and has a kitchen at your disposal

instead.

Prices range from ¥1,000 to ¥26,000 but within these wide price bands there is a whole host of different services offered by each accommodation so make sure you read the individual details of each entry. The list here is selective and there are many perfectly good places which did not make this guide but I have tried to include a broad mixture of accommodation based on good service and reputation.

Often prices are based on breakfast and dinner included and the price can be reduced if you opt not to have your meals at the accommodation but be aware that outside of the main villages you may need your own transport to find a restaurant.

PLACES OF INTEREST

Yakushima is blessed with stunning mountain ranges and world class hiking trails so when most people come to Yakushima they quite rightly head straight up the mountains, but there is more than meets the eye to the overgrown vegetation that lines the circular coastal road. I have included therefore a selection of places of interest in the 'WHAT TO DO' sections so you can explore the whole island to your heart's delight.

SPECIALITIES OF YAKUSHIMA

While in Yakushima there are many types of food to try which can only be found on the island or in this area of Japan. The following is a list of popular Yakushima delicacies:

CITRUS FRUIT
- TANKAN (たんかん) are harvested between Feb - March and are a cross between a ponkan and an orange. They are thought to be juicier and sweeter. A box of 15 of either is ¥2,000 and 1 bag at road side shop is ¥200. You can also buy Tankan/Ponkan squeezed juice and ice cream or sorbet.
- PONKAN (ぽんかん) are harvested from Dec - Jan. They are softer than tankan and are thought to have a richer taste.

RICE/ POTATO
- KAKARAN DANGO (かからん団子) is a sticky rice cake made with yomogi (Japanese mugwort) wrapped with a china root leaf. ¥300 for 4.
- YAKUTORO (屋久とろ) are Yam potatoes which are grown in Yakushima. 1 bag for ¥100 - ¥200.

DEER MEAT
- YAKUSHIKA (ヤクシカ) is the local species of deer and you can

try eating this type of venison in many of Yakushima's restaurants.

FLYING FISH

- KUBIORESABA (首折れさば). 'Saba' means mackerel and 'Kubiore' means broken neck. They are so named because as soon as they are caught, their necks are broken to keep them fresh. They can be eaten as raw sashimi or in shabushabu, a boiled stew. The whole fish can be bought for ¥800 at the supermarket and you can ask them to make it into sashimi for free.
- TSUKEAGE (つけ揚げ) is a deep fried Tobiuo (flying fish) fish cake. It costs ¥130 for one Yakuage at Yakushima Kanko Centre restaurant in Miyanoura.
- TOBIUO NO KARAAGE (飛び魚の唐揚げ) is deep fried Tobiuo fish which soaked in light salted water for a night.
- TOBIUO NO ICHIYABOSHI (飛び魚の一夜干し) is Tobiuo fish which has been dried for the night after soaked in salty water. It costs around ¥450.

SHELL-FISH

- TOKOBUSHI (とこぶし) or ISOMON (いそもん) are small abalone and caught at low tide every month. You can see local people scouring the rocks for them with net bags and hooked spears.
- KAME-NO-TE (かめのて) is a shellfish known as 'Se' and is found in April-June. It has the appearance of a turtle's hand hence the name 'kame-no-te' (Turtle's hand).

DRINKS

- PASSION WINE (パッションワイン) is red or white wine made with locally grown passion fruit. ¥950 a bottle (720 ml).
- MITAKE SHOCHU (三岳焼酎) is a distilled alcohol made from sweet potatoes with around 25% alcohol by volume. It is the most popular brand of shochu in Yakushima and when deliveries of the large ¥2,000 bottles arrive in supermarkets, lines form and only one purchase per person is allowed.

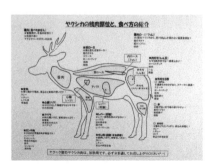

6 FOOD/ACCOMMODATION/SIGHTS
THE NORTH EAST

SHITOGO (志戸子) AREA

WHAT TO DO

SHITOKO GAJYUMARU PARK (志戸子ガジュマル園)
• Signed from the main road at Shitogo (志戸子), 3 km east of Isso. Turn towards the sea, after 200 m turn right and then the park is 300 m ahead. The road is narrow and the car park is next to the sea wall in front of the park.
• Get off at No.14 Shitoko (志戸子) bus stop and walk 200 m towards the sea. At the intersection turn right and the park is 300 m to the right.
    Some of the banyan trees here are as old as 500 years and there are plenty of specimens to look at in this small park. There is a Gajyumaru festival held outside the park in May with local food to try. Open April-August 08.30-18.30; Sept-March 08.30-17.00. Price: Adults ¥200 / Students ¥100. Tel: 42-0100.

MIYANOURA (宮之浦) AREA

WHERE TO EAT/DRINK

PACKED LUNCHES or BENTO (弁当)

It is common for hikers to reserve a freshly cooked packed lunch before they go hiking in Yakushima. Should you wish to do the same, you need to order the food the day before and collect it on the way to the mountain in the early hours of the morning. The pick-up time should be arranged when ordering. You can usually order this through your accommodation but here are the main stores that provide this service:

¥ **SHIMAMUSUBI** (島むすび) Tel: 42-0770.
¥ **YAOHACHI** (八百八) Tel: 42-0414.
¥ **ATTAKA BENTO** (あったか弁当) Tel: 42-3222.
Alternatively if you are happy to pick up a packed lunch on the colder side, these have a large selection and are often discounted later in the day:
¥ **A CO-OP** (Aコープ) on the road to Shiratani Unsuikyo.
¥ **WAI WAI LAND** (わいわいランド) on Route 77 opposite the hospital.

BAKERIES

¥ **SHINGETSUDO** (新月堂菓子舗) is next to Minami Nihon Bank (南日本銀行) in the centre of Miyanoura. Tel: 42-0131.
¥ **KIMURAYA** (木村屋) is after Miyanoura Bridge on the left. Tel: 42-0453.
¥ **HIRAMIYA** (凡我堂ひらみ屋) is opposite Yakushima High School (屋久島高校) up the hill (towards Anbo) from Miyanoura river. Tel: 42-2056.

RESTAURANTS/CAFES

¥¥ **YAKUSHIMA GALLERY REST CAFE** (レスト屋久島) is in the Yakushima Kanko Center (屋久島観光センター), a two-floored lime green building close to the entrance of the port. Serves a set breakfast and lunch. Price: Lunch ~ ¥1,000; Dinner ~ ¥2,000. Hours: 09.30 - 15.30; summer season also 17.30 – 21.00. Tel: 42-0091.
¥ **GUROSU CURRY HOUSE** (グロース) is located next to Miyanoura River opposite the small river-side rest area. It appears more like a bar than a traditional restaurant but the curry is good. English menu. Price: ~ ¥1,000. Hours: 11.00 - 15.00 and 19.00 - 03.00. Tel: 42-2650.

¥¥ RESTAURANT TERADAYA (レストラン洋食寺田屋) is on the main road in Miyanoura opposite another listed restaurant, Yakiniku Ippudo. It is midway between Miyanoura River and the Port on the sea side of the main road and serves set meals. Price: Dinner ~ ¥2,000. Hours: 11.00-14.00 & 17.30-21.00. Closed Sat. Tel: 49-1117

¥ MAM'S KITCHEN （屋久島まむずきっちん）is on the mountain side of Route 77 heading northwards out of Miyanoura. Fresh home-made 'salted' cookies, cakes and ice cream. Price: ~ ¥1,000. Hours: Mid-summer (mid-July – mid-Aug) open every day, otherwise open Mon, Tues, Frid & Sat 09.00-17.00. Winter months only open Tues, Frid & Sat 10.00-14.00. Tel: 42-2822. Web: https://mams-kitchen.jimdo.com/english

¥ PANORAMA (パノラマ) is a stylish new cafe/restaurant and offers a great mixture of food from modern to traditional. It is in the center of Miyanoura on the second turning from the river. Kagoshima Bank (鹿児島銀行) is on the corner and the road is cobbled. English menu. Price: ~ ¥1,000. Hours: Lunch 11.00 – 14.00; Dinner 17.00 – 23.00. Closed on Wed. Tel: 42-0400.

¥¥ SHIOSAI (潮騒) serves Japanese food and has a great reputation for its seafood. It is on the sea side of the main road in Miyanoura closer to the port entrance than the river. Price: Lunch ~ ¥2,000; Dinner ~ ¥2,000. Hours: 11.30 – 14.00; 17.30 – 21.30. Closed Thurs. Tel: 42-2721.

¥¥ FURUSATOICHIBA (ふるさと市場) has a wide selection of food and is a good choice if you are not sure what food to eat. They serve flying fish and Yakushima food as well as noodles and rice dishes. It is opposite the park at the entrance to the port. The front section is a large souvenir shop but the back section is a restaurant with solid Yakusugi tables. Price: Lunch ~ ¥2,000. Hours: 08.00 – 15.00. Tel: 42-3333 Web: yakushima.co.jp/ichiba

¥ KAEDEAN (楓庵) Serves Japanese noodles (soba and udon) near Nakagawa Sports store on the main road in Miyanoura, midway between the river and the port entrance. Closed Sun. Price: ~ ¥1,000. Hours: 11.00 – 15.30. Tel: 42-0398.

¥¥ YAKINIKU IPPUDO (焼肉一風堂) is a large restaurant serving yakiniku (fried meat that you cook yourself on a flat plate at your table). It is midway between Miyanoura River and the Port on the sea side of the main road in a traditional building. Look for the orange signs. Price: Lunch ~ ¥1,000; Dinner ~ ¥3,000. Hours: 11.00-14.00 & 17.00-22.00. Closed Wed. Tel: 42-1220.

¥¥ SUSHI WAKASHIO (鮨若潮) serves locally caught sushi and is very popular. It is in the centre of Miyanoura, one street inland from Nakagawa Sports on Route 77. Price: ~ ¥3,000 Hours: 17.00 – 22.00. Closed Tues. Tel: 42-2114

¥¥ **RYUHOU** (龍鳳) offers Chinese food like noodles and fried rice – eat in or take away. It is at the end of the main pedestrian road parallel to the river, at the opposite end to the two banks, and close to the shrine. Price: ~ ¥3,000. Tel: 42-0825 Closed on Sun. Hours: 11.00–14.00 & 18.00–21.00.

¥ **WANRON** (王龍) is a small Chinese restaurant serving ramen noodles, fried rice and gyoza (fried dumplings). There are pictures of the menu on the wall to choose from. Serves black pork ramen (黒豚角煮ラーメン), a local dish. It is opposite Miyanoura Elementary school just before the river (from Anbo direction). Price: ~ ¥1,000. Hours: 11.00-21.00 Tel: 42-1222

¥ **YAKUSHIMA SHOKUDOU** (やくしま食堂) is on the corner of Route 77 and the river in the center of Miyanoura. It serves a Yakushima speciality set, curry and ramen noodles. Also tea, coffee, smoothies and beer on tap. English menu available. Price: ~ ¥1,500. Serves breakfast, lunch and dinner. Tel: 42-1868.

¥¥ **E. THE CAFE GANTA** (いざカフェがん太) is located by Miyanoura River and is popular with a cross section of people. Food is standard Izakaya　(居酒屋) fayre but also has flying fish. Price: ~ ¥3,000. Closed on the 1st and 3rd Sunday of the month. 18.00 – 02.00. Tel: 42-2015.

WHERE TO STAY

¥ **OCEANVIEW CAMPSITE** (オーシャンビューキャンプ場) is on the south side of the river. Turn towards the sea at Miyanoura Elementary school and turn right before the port. By bus get off at No.31 Miyanoura Sho-mae (宮之浦小前) bus stop. Price: Camping is ¥800 pp/n and tents can be rented for ¥1,200 pp/n ~. Check in: 14.00-19.00. Check out: 12.00. You can reserve a place at the Yakushima Kanko Centre (屋久島観光センター) near the port entrance in Miyanoura. Tel: 42-0091 Web: y-ovc.com

¥ **KAIRAKUEN CAMPSITE & MINSHUKU** (民宿海楽園キャンプ場) is close to No.33 Eidan (営団) bus stop. Turn towards the sea just before Miyanoura hospital (屋久島徳州会病院) and Wai Land supermarket (coming from Miyanoura direction) and continue to the end (the cliff top). Price: Camping is ¥800 pp/n, ¥100 for a shower and rental bungalows for ¥1,200 pp/n. Check out: 10.00. The minshuku is from ¥3,500 pp/n without meals. Tel: 42-0269 Web: e-yakushima.jp

¥ **YAKUSHIMA YOUTH HOSTEL** (屋久島ユースホステル）is conveniently placed near the center of Miyanoura. At the port entrance there is a park with toilets and picnic tables. Follow the road that runs at the other side of the park. The youth hostel is a short walk on the left.

Rooms are clean and well-organised, there is free Wi-Fi and a terrace looking over the port. English speaking staff. Price: ¥2,700 pp/n ~ (YH member) or ¥3,300 pp/n ~ (Non-member). Book directly in English on their website. Tel: 49-1316 Web: yakushima-yh.net Email: yakushimayyh@gmail.com

¥ **SUDOMARI MINSHUKU FRIEND** (素泊まり民宿ふれんど) is conveniently located directly on Route 77 in the middle of Miyanoura. Although it appears rather weathered, this guesthouse has a certain charm about it that is sometimes lacking in newer accommodation. They offer private rooms for up to 5 people with beds or with tatami mats. Price: A twin room should cost ¥6,480 ~ (total) and there are also male and female dorms for ¥3,240 ~ pp/n. Book directly in English on booking.com.

¥¥¥ **SEASIDE HOTEL YAKUSHIMA** (シーサイドホテル屋久島) is a large older hotel close to the port with its entrance before you reach the Yakushima Environmental Culture Village Centre from the Port Terminal. It is popular with tour groups. Price: ¥13,650 ~ pp/n. Tel: 42-0175 Web: www.ssh-yakushima.co.jp Email: yoyaku@ssh-yakushima.co.jp. You can also book via any of the large hotel finder websites i.e. booking.com or travel.rakuten.co.jp

WHAT TO DO

MIYANOURA VILLAGE (宮之浦)

The village of Miyanoura is the principal settlement on the island with more than 20% of Yakushima's population and is dominated by its two main industries: the Port and the silicon carbide factory owned by Yakushima Denko, an ugly collection of smoking rusty buildings on the hillside in the town centre. It is well worth wandering around to get the feel of the place but it is not the prettiest of villages – for beauty look beyond to the mountains.

¥ **YAKUSHIMA ENVIRONMENTAL CULTURE VILLAGE CENTER** (屋久島環境文化村センター)

• On the corner of the main intersection to the port. There is a car park at the rear.

• Get off at No.20 Miyanoura Port Entrance (宮之浦港入口) bus stop and walk towards the entrance of the port.

Free to enter but to watch the documentary: Adults ¥520, High school/ college ¥360, Elementary/Junior High ¥260 and under 6 are free. Hours: 09.00-17.00. Closed on 3rd Tues every moth. Web: yakushima.

or.jp/english Tel: 42-2900

If you want to get your bearings or if the weather takes a turn for the worse, this a nice little exhibition and has a 250-seat wide screen cinema showing a nature documentary of the island (shown about 8 times a day). It also serves as an information centre for hiking in the mountains and the staff should speak some English.

¥ YAKUSHIMA TOWN HISTORY AND FOLK MUSEUM (屋久島町歴史民俗資料館)

• Turn towards the mountains at the traffic signals north of Miyanoura River. Continue parallel to the river for 1 min and then it is on your left before you reach the end of the road.

• Get off at No.23 Miyanoura (宮之浦) bus stop and turn inland along the road running directly parallel to the river. (Do not cross the bridge). The museum is on your left after a 5 min walk.

The museum exhibits illustrate the history of the life of islanders and is an interesting detour if the weather keeps you off the mountains. Price: Adults ¥100, Children ¥50. Hours: 09.00-17.00 Closed Mon, Sat afternoons and on New Year holidays Tel: 42-1900

¥ YAKUSHIMA COMPREHENSIVE NATURE PARK (屋久島総合自然公園)

• In Miyanoura, take Route 594 heading to Shiratani Unsuikyo. Go past A Co-op supermarket, cross the bridge and as the road curves there is a small parking area with drinking water on the right. The road next to this leads, after around a 5 min drive, to the car park on your right.

• Get off at No.31 Miyanoura-sho-mae (宮之浦小前) bus stop and take the mountain road towards Shiratani Unsuikyo. After crossing a river the road steeply rises and bends. Turn right at the sign for Yakushima Comprehensive Nature Park (屋久島総合自然公園) and the car park is at the end of the road (30 min).

There are essentially 2 parts to the park here, either side of the main road. One is the Yaseishokubutsuen (野生植物園) which is across the road from the car park, further away from the river. It has many of the

plants and flowers that naturally grow in Yakushima in greenhouses or display areas. Hours: 8.30-17.00. Price: Adults ¥300, Children ¥100. Tel: 42-2727

The other part of the park surrounds the car park and is free of charge. It is nicely kept and there are two main paths that lead you around past the open air stage. The river next to the park can be found running along the far side. Find the wooden walkway and at some point you will find a gap in the trees so you can get to the rocks by the river. Have a dip in the crystal clear water or spot the odd monkey in the trees on the opposite bank, bring a picnic and relax. In late May, you may be lucky enough to see the thousands of fireflies that come out at night here in the park.

¥ YUNOKO NO YU ONSEN (ゆのこの湯)

This hot spring is actually in Yakushima Comprehensive Nature Park (屋久島総合自然公園) as detailed above. It is fairly new and run by the authorities in Miyanoura. You should reserve one of the baths before

16.00 but after this time it is open for all. The water is artificially heated via a wood burner out back. Price: ¥400. Hours: 12.00 – 19.00. Tel: 42-0305. Closed on Monday. There is usually a caretaker at the Onsen who you can book with.

RYUJINSUGI TRAIL (R1)

This trail begins further along the road that led you to Yakushima Comprehensive Nature Park. If you continue straight (not over the bridge) then you come to Ryujin sugi Trail Entrance (龍神杉登山口) and from there it is a long 7.5 hour round-trip hike. More details in the RYUJINSUGI TRAIL (R1) section.

ROUTE 594

If you follow Route 594 from Miyanoura upwards, you steeply climb along a road which hangs at the side of the mountain. It has been much improved, but there is still a section higher up where it is a single track. Watch out for buses which regularly take this route.

After driving for 30 min, you come to SHIRATANI UNSUIKYO (S1) Entrance on your right and then cross a bridge before arriving at the car park. From then on the road is blocked. In the winter months and during Rainy season (May-July), Route 594 can either be blocked with snow or flooded and a barrier across the road will prevent you from going any further. Check whether the road is open during these months.

KUSUGAWA (楠川) AREA

WHERE TO EAT/DRINK

¥ **MARUYA CAFE** (マルヤカフェ) serves drinks and a set lunch in a small roadside cabin. If the weather is good, you can sit outside. If not there are 4 seats inside at the counter. Price: Lunch ~ ¥1,000. Hours: 10.00 – 17.00. Closed on Tues and Wed. Tel: 43-5565.

WHERE TO STAY

¥¥ **OCEAN VIEW GUEST HOUSE** (オーシャンビューゲストハウス) is a rental cottage towards the mountain in Kusugawa. It is in a secluded setting in the woods next to a tea plantation and has two beds, a fridge and kettle but no kitchen. Ideal if you have a car rental. Guest collection from/to the port. English spoken. Price: ¥10,500 ~ a night. Minimum 2 night stay. Book directly on Airbnb.com.

¥¥ **MINSHUKU SHIRATANI** (民宿白谷) is in Kusugawa, coming from Miyanoura take the last left before the river and it is on the corner. It offers 7 rooms with air-con, toilets and TV. Bathrooms are shared and it has an open-air stone bath hut with sea views. Price: ¥5,940 ~ pp/n with breakfast. Tel: 42-0809 Web: seaforest.info. You can book via any of the large hotel finder websites i.e. booking.com or travel.rakuten.co.jp.

WHAT TO DO

¥ **KUSUGAWA ONSEN** (楠川温泉)

This hot spring is signposted towards the mountains on Route 77 in Kusugawa. It has the feel of a local onsen with a small bath which means only a handful of people at a time can bathe. It is artificially heated using water from an alkaline cold spring. You need to bring everything you need to wash with. Price: ¥300. Hours: 09.00 – 20.00. Tel: 42-1166.

¥¥ **YAWARACA 'THE SCENT OF YAKUSHIMA LAB'** (島の香りラボやわら香) is on the mountain side of Route 77 in Kusugawa. By bus get off at No.39 Shimo-makino (下牧野) bus stop. They sell essential oils which you can mix yourself, small craft items and have aroma-massage treatments at SPA KIOKU, a separate purpose-built cabin. You can buy their products online here: http://yawaraca.shop-pro.jp. Hours: 09:00 - 18:30. Closed Wed and Thurs. (Spa: 09.00 – 21.00; Closed Thurs). Prices for aroma-treatments: from ¥2,000 for 15 min to ¥30,000 for 2 people for 2 hours. Web: yawaraca.jp. Email: info@yawaraca.jp. Tel: 42-0109.

KOSEDA (小瀬田) AREA

WHERE TO EAT/DRINK

¥¥¥ **IL MARE** (イルマーレ) serves authentic Italian food in form of pizza, pasta and set menus. On Route 77, 100 m north of the airport in Koseda. Price: Lunch ~ ¥2,000; Dinner ~ ¥5,000. Hours: 11.30 - 14.30 & 18.00 - 20.30. Tel: 43-5666 Web: ilmare3.jp

¥ **KISSA JURIN** (喫茶樹林) Good for light meals (toast, salad, coffee etc.). Head from the airport towards Miyanoura and turn left just before 'au' & Some's store, it is 100 m from the turn off. Price: Lunch ~ ¥1,000. Hours: 10.00 - 17.00. Closed Sun. Tel: 43-5454 Web: jurinn.com

¥ **AIKOTEI** (あいこ亭) has its own entrance within the Airport Hotel (屋久島エアポートホテル) next to the airport. Has various set meals for lunch and dinner including steak. Price: Lunch ~ ¥1,000; Dinner ~ ¥2,000. Hours: 11.30 - 14.00 & 17.00 - 20.30. Tel: 43-5788.

¥¥ **LA MONSTERA** (ラモンステラ) serves stuffed rice omelettes with home-farmed eggs. It is a short way from the airport on the sea side of the main road (Anbo direction), close to the lighthouse. Price: Lunch ~ ¥2,000. Hours: Only open 11.30-16.00 on Thurs, Frid & Sat. Tel: 43-5080.

¥ **HIBISCUS** (ハイビスカス) serves curry in many shapes and forms – seafood, hamburger, cutlet, vegetable etc. It is close to La Monstera above on the sea side of the main road south from Koseda. Price: Lunch ~ ¥1,000. Free Wi-Fi. Hours: 11.00-17.00. Tel: 43-5195.

WHERE TO STAY

¥ **RIDER HOUSE TOMARIGI** (ライダーハウスとまり木) is close to the airport in Koseda. At the airport intersection turn inland and go along the small road that runs next to Jomon-No-Yado Manten (まんてん). Friendly and very relaxed atmosphere with Wi-Fi. Price: ¥2,000 ~ pp/n with breakfast and you can pitch a tent for ¥800. Tel: 43-5069 Web: yakushima-tomarigi.jp. You can also book via any of the large hotel finder websites i.e. booking.com or travel.rakuten.co.jp

¥¥¥ **COTTAGE ORANGE HOUSE YAKUSHIMA** (コテージ オレンジハウス屋久島) offers an annex cottage next to the owner's residence on a quiet side road close to Route 77. Heading northwards, it is the first turning towards the mountains after the traffic signals at the airport intersection in Koseda. Set in a spacious garden and with free Wi-Fi.

Price: ¥19,440 ~ for 2 nights for 2 people. Email: taiichi@gmail.com Web: www13.plala.or.jp/pochix/orangehouseEn.html. Tel/Fax: 0997-43-5755. Book via any of the large hotel finder websites i.e. booking.com or travel.rakuten.co.jp

¥¥¥ JOMON-NO-YADO MANTEN （縄文の宿まんてん）is a resort hotel right across the road from the airport. It boasts a large onsen and buffet restaurant. Price: ¥16,200 ~ pp/n. Tel: 43-5751 Web: www.arm-manten.co.jp. You can also book via any of the large hotel finder websites i.e. booking.com or travel.rakuten.co.jp

WHAT TO DO

¥¥ JOMON-NO-YADO MANTEN ONSEN (縄文の宿 まんてん温泉)

This hot spring is inside Jomon-No-Yado Manten hotel as detailed above. Price includes towel, yukata, soap, shampoo and use of the relaxation room with comfy massage chairs. Outdoor/indoor bath. The water is partly artificially heated using water from an alkaline hot spring. Hours: 10.30-22.30. Price: Adult: ¥1,600 / Child: ¥1,000. Tel: 43-5751 Web: www.arm-manten.co.jp

AIKO DAKE TRAIL (A2) starts in the mountains behind Koseda. It is a 6-hour round trip and the trail is steep but if this does not put you off, you can find more details in the AIKO DAKE TRAIL section.

PILLOW-SHAPED LAVA BEACH (枕状溶岩)

• The beach is signed towards the sea 1 km south of Nagakubo village (永久保) and 4 km north of Anbo (安房). There is a small parking area where the two tracks start at the end of the road.

• Get off at No.57 Kuwano (桑野) bus stop then walk towards the sea at the turn-off.

The narrow road is lined by trees and after 700 m makes a sharp turn to the right. It then descends very steeply for 300 m as it winds itself down to the coast. At the bottom there are two tracks going in opposite directions. Left will take you 200 m to Tashiro Beach (田代海岸) a quiet sandy beach, frequented by turtles in hatching season, and right 100 m to the fascinating lava rock formations.

The natural process of lava being cooled by the sea and then fresh lava breaking the newly formed crust and squeezing out more boiling material have created what are supposed to look like folded pillows, hence the name.

7 Food/Accommodation/Sights
The South East

ANBO (安房) AREA

WHERE TO EAT/DRINK

PACKED LUNCHES or BENTO (弁当)

¥ **ASAHI BENTO** (あさひ弁当) Tel: 46-4007.
¥ **DEKITATEYA** (できたて屋) Tel: 46-3071.
¥ **SHIMASHIMA KITCHEN** (島・しまキッチン) on the mountain side of Route 77 near the Panchiko parlor in Anbo. They serve freshly-made takeaway food. Price: ~ ¥1,000. Hours: 11:00 - 18:00. Closed Sun and holidays.

BAKERIES

¥ **SHIIBA** (しいば) is north of, and on the same side as, the turn off for Yakusugiland on Route 77. It offers a wide selection of bread, sandwiches and cakes. Tel: 46-2067.

RESTAURANTS/CAFES

¥ **MOSSBURGER** is a national fast food chain and sits on Route 77 close to Anbo River. It serves burgers, fries and all things fast. Price: ~ ¥1,000. Hours: 10.00 – 22.00. The Mossburger car park is 50 m up the hill on the right.

¥ **YORONZAKA** (よろん坂) is on the mountain side of the hill heading south out of Anbo. It has free Wi-Fi and is a cafe at lunchtime and a bar at night. Very friendly, very relaxed and a warm welcome to foreign visitors (little English though!). Price: ~ ¥1,000. Hours: 11.00 - 23.00 Web: Tel: 46-2949

¥¥ **RESTAURANT SAN PAULO** (レストランサンパウロ) is a 'family restaurant' with a wide selection of set meals and their own brand of salad dressing. It is close to Anbo Jetfoil Port, 200 m down the hill from the post office. Price: ~ ¥2,000. Hours: 10.00 - 15.00 & 17.30 - 22.00. Closed 1st & 3rd Tues of the month. Tel: 46-3848. Web: www.sanpauro.com

¥ **SMILEY** (スマイリー) makes their own cakes and sandwiches in a small friendly cafe by Anbo River. Signed on the river road between the fishing port and Anbo Bridge. Price: ~ ¥1,000. Hours: 11.00 - 18.00. Closed on Tues. Web: cafe-smiley.info Tel: 46-2853

¥¥ **SANPOTEI** (散歩亭) is a modern Izakaya pub run by young staff with a wide selection of food and music. There is a cosy back section often playing jazz. It has a fantastic riverside setting near Manten Bridge (まんてん橋), the old Anbo Bridge, on the opposite side of the river. Price: ~ ¥2,000. Hours: 11.30 – 15.00 (lunch), 18.00 - 01.00. Closed on Sun. Tel: 46-2905. Web: http://st-pote.sakura.ne.jp

¥ **KITCHEN HOUSE KATAGIRI** (キッチンハウスかたぎり) offers set lunch menus, pasta and curry. It is on the sea side of Route 77 near the traffic signals heading north out of Anbo. Hours: 11.00 – 21.00. Closed on Sun. Price: ~ ¥1,500. Tel: 46-4282.

¥ **FAMILY RESTAURANT KAMOGAWA** (ファミリーレストランかもがわ) is on Route 77 in the center directly across the road from Mossburger. It serves good quality rice and noodle dishes, is cheap and has an English menu. Hours: 09.00 – 15.00; 17.00 - 21.00. Closed Sun. Price: ~ ¥1,000. Tel: 46-2101.

¥ **FOOD SHOP AWAHO** (フードショップあわほ) is in the center of Anbo, a few hundred meters along the side road that is next to Mossburger. It sells freshly made bento boxes and simple classic Japanese dishes. You can buy a bento box and eat it there or order from the menu.

Free Wi-Fi. Price: ~ ¥1,000. Tel: 46-2605.

¥¥ **YAKUDON** (屋久どん) serves a good selection of local Yakushima food such as flying fish. Very popular and scenic setting by the sea. Close to Anbo port, follow the road past A Co-op and it is on the sea side of the road after the car park and toilets. Price: Lunch ~ ¥2,000; Dinner ~ ¥2,000. Hours: 11.00 - 15.00; 18.00 – 21.00. Web: yakushima-net.com/restaurant.html Tel: 46-3210.

¥¥ **HANASATUKI** (花皐月) is a small traditional restaurant offering yakiniku and a selection of local food. Turn inland at the intersection after the Green Hotel (coming from Miyanoura direction) and it is 100 m on the right. Price: Dinner ~ ¥3,000. Web: yakushima-hanastk.com Tel: 46-3687.

¥¥¥ **SUSHI ISONOKAORI** (寿司 いその香り) is a very popular restaurant serving sushi and sashimi on the mountain side of Route 77 on the way into Anbo from Miyanoura. Price: Lunch ~ ¥2,000; Dinner ~ ¥4,000. Hours: 11.30-14.00 & 18.00-22.00. Closed Tues. Tel: 46-3218

¥ **BANRAIKEN** (萬来軒) is a busy Chinese restaurant with large servings. It specialises in ramen noodles but also has a section offering sushi. It is a few doors away from Anbo post office up the hill from the port. Price: ~ ¥1,000. Hours: 11.00-15.00 & 17.30-21.30. Closed every 2nd Thursday. Tel: 46-2109

¥¥ **JIIJI YA** (じいじ家) is next to Anbo river, close to Manten Bridge (まんてん橋), the old Anbo bridge. They serve traditional Yakushima food and it is a good place to try black pork and Kubioresaba (首折れさば), locally caught mackerel. Price: Lunch ~ ¥1,000; Dinner ~ ¥3,000. Hours: 11.30 – 14.00, 18.00 – 23.00. Web: https://ji-jiya.jimdo.com Tel: 46 3087.

¥ **SUGI-NO-CHAYA** (杉の茶屋) serves light meals like noodles and rice balls for lunch. It has a rustic setting in the forest in the grounds of

the Yakusugi museum. Price: ~ ¥1,000. Hours: 10.00-14.00. Closed the first Tues every month. Tel: 46-2484.

WHERE TO STAY

¥¥ **MORI-NO-KOKAGE** (森のこかげ) is signed on the main road just north of Anbo. Turn towards the sea and it is 100 m on the left. Run by a welcoming English speaker, it offers clean homemade wooden cabins, a hammock to swing on and barbecue facilities. Great attention to detail. ¥4,250 ~ pp/n Tel: 9060017512. Email: oshirase@morinokokage. net Web: morinokokage.net (English). You can also book via any of the large hotel finder websites i.e. booking.com or travel.rakuten.co.jp

¥ **BANYAMINE CAMPSITE** (番屋峯キャンプ場) is beside Yaku-don (屋久どん) restaurant overlooking the harbour in Anbo. From the jet foil port turn right, go past A Co-op supermarket (on your left) and after the parking area with toilets (on your right) turn right down to a collection of buildings by the sea. The campsite is at the end of these buildings, the last one of which is Yakudon restaurant. Tents and camping equipment can be rented. Open all year round. Price: ¥500 pp/n + tent price from ¥200. Shower for ¥500 (20 mins). Tel: 46-3210 FAX: 46-2955

¥ **HANASATSUKI** (花皐月) is near Anbo Elementary School (安房小学校). Turn towards the mountains at the large hall and police station (屋久島警察署) and then take the second right. It is on this road after a few minutes. Price: ¥3,000 ~ pp/n (April-Oct) and ¥2,500 ~ (Nov-March) or if you have a sleeping bag ¥2,000 ~ pp/n. Web: Yakushima-hanastk. com Tel: 46-3687/ 09095668517

¥ **YUKAINA NAKAMATACHI BACKPACKERS HOUSE** (素泊ま

り民宿ゆかいな仲間たち) consists of conveniently placed basic dorms above Moss burger near the river. Rooms have air-conditioning and there is a common area with a simple kitchen. Hot showers and free Wi-Fi. ¥2,800 ~ p/n. Book direct via booking.com. TEL + FAX: 46-3661.

¥ **MORI-NO-KIRAMEKI** (森のきらめき) is on Route 77 at the intersection at the top of the hill in the center of Anbo. Downstairs is an outdoors store and upstairs is Conveni-lodge (コンビニロッジ) which consists of en-suite dorms with clean wooden bunks. Free Wi-Fi. Price: ¥3,500 ~ pp/n. Web: morinokirameki.com. Book direct via booking.com Tel: 49-7101.

¥ **DAICHAN HOUSE** (大ちゃんハウス) offers rooms in real Mongol huts, a curious hybrid between camping and staying in a hostel. It is on Route 77 heading south out of Anbo. Climb the long hill and at the very top as it bends, look for the sign on the left. It may look a little worse for wear but the owner is reported to be very helpful and I hear nothing but good reviews from people who have stayed there. Price: ¥3,150 ~ pp/n. Book via any of the large hotel finder websites i.e. booking.com or travel.rakuten.co.jp. TEL + FAX: 46-3565

¥ **MINSHUKU SUIMEISO** (民宿水明荘) sits beside Anbo river, further inland than Manten bridge (まんてん橋) [the older of the two Anbo bridges]. It is on the second road up running parallel to the river. Japanese film director Hayao Miyazaki is reputed to love this minshuku when he was here researching for his movie, Princess Mononoke. It is showing its age now so do not expect luxury but it is as authentic as it gets and has a great old onsen bathroom. Price: ¥3,500 ~ pp/n without meals and ¥6,800 ~ with two meals. Book via any of the large hotel finder websites i.e. booking.com or travel.rakuten.co.jp. Tel: 46-2078.

¥ **MINSHUKU TOROKKO NO YADO** (トロッコの宿) offers 10 clean but small bunk bed rooms on the corner of a side road in the center of Anbo, near the fire station. Follow the road at the side of Mossburger to the end and it is on the corner to your left. No free Wi-Fi. Rooms have air conditioning and TV and kettles/hairdryers can be borrowed at no extra charge. Bathroom is shared. It is all new, basic and cheap. Price: ¥3,100 ~ pp/n. Tel: 46-2633. Web: torokkonoyado.jimdo.com. Book via any of the large hotel finder websites i.e. booking.com or travel.rakuten. co.jp.

¥ **GUESTHOUSE DREAM** (ゲストハウスドリーム) offers simple rooms above Food Shop Awaho (フードショップあわほ) in the center of Anbo. Take the side road next to Mossburger and it is on your left after 200 m. There is a small seated communal area with a fridge and kettle. Price: ¥3,000 ~ pp/n. The longer you stay, the cheaper per night. Tel: 46-2605. You can book in Food Shop Awaho.

¥ **ICHIGO ICHIE** (一期一会) is next to Anbo Elementary school (安房小学校) on the road running uphill parallel with the river from Anbo intersection. The road is directly opposite Mori-no-kirameki (森のきらめき) outdoor store and hostel on Route 77. It is a traditional small guesthouse near a path down to the river. Price: ¥4,000 ~ pp/n or ¥7,000 ~ pp/n with 2 meals. TEL: 46-3550. You can book in Food Shop Awaho (フードショップあわほ) in Anbo.

¥ **MINSHUKU TAKENKO** (民宿たけんこ) is renowned for good food and clean rooms. Turn towards the mountain from Route 77 at the first traffic signals as you come into Anbo (from Miyanoura direction). There is a gas station on one corner. Go straight and as the road bends sharply to the left, turn right. It is soon after on your left. Price: ¥3,500 ~ pp/n. Tel: 46-3382 Web: www17.plala.or.jp/takenko

¥¥ **TABIBITO-NO-YADO MANMARU** (旅人の宿まんまる) has rooms laid out motel style around an open area and at one end a large communal bath, the other the restaurant. Very friendly with English spoken and close to the port. Follow the road running behind A Co-op, go through the short tunnel and it is on the left. Price: ¥8,800 ~ with 2 meals. Tel: 45-2137. Book direct in English on their website. Web: http://manmaru-yakushima.com (English) Email: info@guesthouse-manmaru.com

¥¥¥ **YAKUSHIMA GREEN HOTEL** （屋久島グリーンホテル）is on Route 77 at the north end of Anbo. It has a spa with a hot stone massage and an artificially heated onsen. ¥10,500 ~ pp/n. Tel: 46-3021 Web: yakushima-gh.com/index.html. You can also book via any of the large hotel finder websites i.e. booking.com or travel.rakuten.co.jp

WHAT TO DO

ANBO (安房)

Anbo is the second main settlement after Miyanoura and has a thriving fishing port and farming industry. It is an interesting place to wander around and look at the weather beaten stores.

Head to the river area and you will pass a small shrine called Jochiku Tomari Mausoleum (如竹神社) dedicated to a Confucian scholar named Jochiku Tomari, the priest who has the dubious honour of encouraging local people to cut down their previously revered trees. (See 'the Forest' section for more details).

There is a local dance in Anbo which has been passed down generation to generation for 300 years called the 'Jochiku Odori' dance to

celebrate his actions.

ANBO PORT (安房港)

- Follow signs to the Jetfoil port and park in the car park nearby.
- Get off at No.64 Anbo port (安房港) bus stop.

This is home to the jetfoil but across from its pink terminal is one of the most important industries in Yakushima and in early afternoon is a hive of activity. This is the main fishing cooperative for 'Tobiuo' (飛び魚) otherwise known as flying fish. Over 1,000 tons of flying fish are caught here over the year and as much as 70% of all the flying fish sold in the markets of Japan are from here. There are over 30 different kinds of flying fish around Japan and most pass by Yakushima on the Kuroshio Current but the most common types are the blue tobiuo (青トビウオ) and the 'semi' tobiuo (セミトビウオ). These can be found within 40 km from Yakushima's shores (See the 'Fauna' section for more details).

ANBO RIVER (安房川)

- Anbo is at the mouth of the river. Parking is not easy around it though. Try the narrow river road near Manten bashi (the older of the two bridges) or find a place nearer the port and walk.
- Get off at No.66 Anbo (安房) bus stop and the river is very close.

The river is stunning in places and is so clear that the boulders deep below on the river bed appear as dark shadows.

At the first sharp bend, there is a sand bank to the right (depending on the tide) and this is a good stopping point if only to swing on the rope and splash into the river. Around the next bend, there is a channelled river which flows strongly from the left and the small stony beach area to the right is also a good stopping point.

The bridge ahead is the 75 m high Matsumine Oh-hashi Bridge (松峯大橋) - a local suicide spot - and all around is thick forest. Soon after you paddle under the bridge the rocks become larger and it is difficult to continue without carrying the kayak. It is still possible to continue but most people turn back soon after the bridge.

A flat boat, Anbo gawa Nagarebune (安房川流れ船), can also be hired for an evening cruise along the river.

HARUTAHAMA BEACH (春田浜海水浴場)

- Signed on the main road near Anbo Bridge (安房橋). Turn towards the sea at the traffic signals and it is then a 5 min drive until a left turn at the small cement works. After 100 m there is a small car park next to the river.

• Get off at No.66 Anbo (安房) bus stop, walk across Anbo Bridge and turn left at the lights. Follow the road as it rises and then falls and continue parallel to the sea for 1.2 km until a left turn after the small cement works. The beach is then 100 m ahead.

Cross the small concrete bridge to the protected swimming area formed using the natural shape of the rocks. The pool has a life guard in the summer months and is a popular place to swim. The toilets and changing rooms are open July and August (09.30 - 17.30).

There is no sandy beach here but do not be put off - instead there is a carpet of jagged dead coral with rock pools full of fascinating sea creatures. Bring appropriate footwear to clamber over the coral and head past the natural swimming pool to the area beyond.

¥ YAKUSUGI MUSEUM (屋久島町立屋久杉自然館)

• Take the mountain road to Yakusugiland (Route 592) for a few kilometers and you will be greeted with the large car park of Yakusugi museum on your left.

• Take any of the Yakusugiland/Kigensugi buses. Get off at No.68 Yakusugi Shizenkan (屋久杉自然館) bus stop. The entrance is behind the trees. Price: Adults ¥600, High school students ¥400, Junior High/ Elementary students ¥300 Hours: 09.00 - 17.00. Closed on the 1st Tuesday of every month and New Year Holidays Tel: 46-3113.

The museum is set in large grounds with paths leading into a short circular forest walk. Inside it has displays about the forest including the 'Branch of life' exhibition (いのちの枝) featuring a branch from Jomon Sugi which snapped under the weight of snow in Dec 2005. There is also a pleasant cafe at the right entrance from the car park called Sugi-no-chaya (杉の茶屋) which is situated in thick forest.

Within the same grounds are two other buildings:

YAKUSHIMA WORLD HERITAGE CONSERVATION CENTER (屋久島世界遺産センター)

This free permanent exhibition has display panels and objects you can touch and feel related to nature in Yakushima. It also serves as an information point for hiking and climbing in the mountains. If you are visiting the museum it is well worth the short walk. Hours: 09.00-17.00 & March - Nov open every day, Dec – Feb open every Sat, and closed for New Year Holidays. Tel: 46-2992 Web: yakushima.or.jp/english

YAKUSHIMA ENVIRONMENTAL CULTURE RESEARCH CENTER (屋久島環境文化研修センター)

This is next to the conservation centre and is not open to the general public. It provides lecture rooms, accommodation and educational facilities for groups learning about Yakushima and the environment. Hours: 09.00 - 17.00 Tel: 46-2900 Web: yakushima.or.jp/English

ROUTE 592

South of Anbo begins Route 592, the main road to the higher mountains. Go past Yakusugi Museum and continue upwards towards Yakusugiland(Y3), Arakawa Trail (A1), Kigen-sugi tree (See the tree sec-

tion in THE BASICS) and Yodogawa Trail (Y1). The initial part of the road often has monkeys at the roadside and also as you get higher, especially near the intersection for the Arakawa Trail. These monkeys are looking for food but do not feed them as you will be disturbing the natural ecosystem. Note that the side road to the Arakawa Trail is blocked to traffic with a barrier across the road – see A1 Trail for more details.

The higher you get, the more beautiful the views. Be aware that although the road has been widened in many places there are still parts with a single track, and buses take this route several times a day. Use the convex mirrors at the side of the road to check what is coming and be prepared to reverse back. If you keep going past

Yakusugiland, you reach the higher mountains and the road sometimes is bumpy with holes but perfectly drivable. Eventually you will reach **Kigen-sugi** (紀元杉), a 3,000 year old sugi, on the right and there are usually buses which stop here and sometimes groups of tourists. After this, the road snakes up to the **Yodogawa Trail Entrance** and then stops at the toilets. To the left next to the toilets is the end of the Onoaida Trail (O2) and to the right is the Yodogawa Trail (Y1). If you only want to explore a little, you can hike the 75 min round trip to the **Yodogawa Hut** and the river just beyond it. You can get a real sense of the higher trails if you do this. If you wish to go further see the full trail details. Note that in the winter months and during Rainy season (May-July), the road can either be blocked with snow or flooded and a barrier across the road

will prevent you from going any further. Check whether the road is open during these months.

SARUKAWA GAJYUMARU (猿川ガジュマル)

• About 1 km south of the village of Hirano (平野), there is a small wooden sign on the mountain side of the main road. Turn here and after 300 m there is a clearing in the forest on your right to park in.

• Get off at No.81 Nakabashi (中橋) and walk 300 m (Anbo direction) before turning left at the sign or get off at No.80 Shouchugawa (焼酎川) and walk 500 m (Onoaida direction) before turning right.

Follow the small path to the end and it should lead you to the famous gajyumaru or banyan trees to your right. They are very distinctive in appearance because their aerial roots hang down to the ground like tentacles.

¥¥ YAKUSHIMA GREEN HOTEL ONSEN (屋久島グリーンホテル温泉)

This artificial hot spring is located inside Yakushima Green Hotel on the sea side of Route 77 at the northern end of Anbo. It has a hot stone spa and onsen open to the general public. Price: Onsen is ¥648 and the Hot stone Spa (岩盤浴) is ¥1,728 for 70 min. Hours: 06.00 – 09.00; 16.00-23.00. Tel: 46-3021 Web: yakushima-gh.com

MUGIO (麦生) AREA

WHERE TO EAT/DRINK

¥¥¥ VITA KITCHEN (ヴィータキッチン) serves everything from Kagoshima black pork and flying fish to pasta and vegetarian and vegan food. On the mountain side of Route 77 north of Mugio. Get off at No.84 Hotogawa (ホトー川) bus stop which is nearby. Price: Lunch ~ ¥3,000; Dinner ~ ¥5,000. Lunch 11:30 - 15:00; Dinner 18:00 - 21:00 (Reservation required). Closed Wed. Web: http://yakushima-vita.jp (English) Tel: 47-3478.

¥ YAKUSHIMA GELATO SORA UMI (屋久島ジェラート・そらうみ) is a cafe which sells freshly made totally natural ice cream. Inside they also have a hammocks to swing in as your slurp. On the sea side of Route 77 just north of Mugio. Price: ~ ¥1,000. Hours: 13:00 - 17:30. Closed Tues and Wed. Web: yakushimagelato.jp

¥ MUIGOKKO (むいごっ娘) is a tiny wooden hut directly opposite the Botanical Research Park (ボタニカルリサーチパーク) in Mugio. It is easily missed as the sign is small above the door but the food (udon noodles) is cheap and as authentic as it comes. You will not find tourists here. Price: Lunch ~ ¥1,000. Hours: 10.00 – 14.00. Closed Frid.

¥¥¥¥ ANAYA & OKAS are both found in Sankara Hotel & Spa Yakushima (see details below). Anaya is a 'casual' French restaurant which combines local seasonal ingredients with a classic French twist and Okas takes this idea to another level of fine dining and provides an open kitchen where diners can watch the preparation of their exquisite set dishes and get explanations of how the ingredients are blended in English. The menu changes daily. You can find the menus for both at Web: www.sankarahotel-spa.com/en. Price: ¥5,000~ Tel: +81997473488.

WHERE TO STAY

¥¥¥¥ SANKARA HOTEL & SPA YAKUSHIMA (サンカラホテル&スパ屋久島) is a luxurious resort complex set in its own grounds in the forest above Mugio. It boasts a fleet of carts to whisk you from your private lodge to the main building with a world-class French restaurant, swimming pool and massage spa. Exceptional attention to detail and guest care. Follow the signs and turn to the mountain side of Route 77 just north of Mugio. Price: ¥26,000 ~ Tel: +81997473488. Book direct in English. Web: www.sankarahotel-spa.com/en

¥¥¥ COTTAGE HANAMANA (コテージHANAMANA) offers luxurious country-style rooms on the mountain side. By car turn towards the mountain just south of Mugio settlement or get off at No.86 Botanical Research Park (ボタニカルリサーチパーク) bus stop, follow the sign to Senpiro waterfall (千尋の滝) heading inland for about 200 m and then turn left at the pink sign. Offers peaceful surroundings, an open air bath and the possibility to charter the whole house. Price: ¥9,500 ~ pp/n TEL & FAX: 47-3398 Web: hanamana.org Email: catseye@lily.odn.ne.jp. You can also book via any of the large hotel finder websites i.e. booking.com or travel.rakuten.co.jp

¥ GUESTHOUSE YAKUSHIMA (ゲストハウス屋久島) is tucked away on a mountain side road yet still very accessible by car or bus. By car turn towards the mountain before Tainokawa Bridge (鯛の川橋). On the other side of the bridge is the Ponkantankan Center. By bus get off at No.87 Tainokawa bus stop which is close by Ponkantankan Center and Toroki falls. Follow the main road across the bridge and take the first turning up towards the mountain. Keep going up and you will cross Tainokawa River again, Guesthouse Yakushima is soon after on the right. It offers dorms and private rooms in an immaculate condition and a communal area for cooking and relaxing. The owner speaks fluent English and really has laid out everything a traveller could need in Yakushima. Price: ¥3,000 ~. TEL.47-3866 You can book directly at Web: www.guesthouse-yakushima.com/eng/index.html. Email: info@guesthouse-yakushima.com

¥¥ YAKUSHIMA COTTAGE MORI-NO-FAIRY (コテージ森のフェアリー) is a collection of split-level cottages facing the coast on Route 77 just north of Mugio village. Each cottage has two beds downstairs and two futons upstairs and is fully equipped with toiletries, towels and

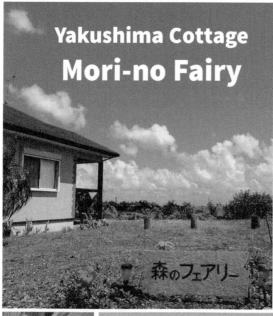

a basic kitchen area. The owners are very welcoming and provide an instruction booklet in English. You can book directly in English at http://morinofairy-y.p2.weblife.me/pg568.html and click on reservations. They offer a discounted rate for booking direct. Price: ¥5,800 ~ pp/n for 2 peo-

Be awakened from your dreams by morning birdsong

Spa treatments to enhance mind, body and soul

 Taste the blessings of heaven earth and ocean.

ple sharing and ¥5,000 ~ pp/n for 3. Email: morinofairy@air.ocn.ne.jp Tel: +81-80-8382-4847.

WHAT TO DO

¥ YAKUSHIMA BOTANICAL RESEARCH PARK (屋久島ボタニカルリサーチパーク)

• A few min south of Mugio, it is clearly signed on the left and the entrance to the car park is from the main road.

• Get off at No.86 Research Park (リサーチパーク) bus stop and it is in front of you, on the sea side of the road.

Popular with tour groups as it also has a restaurant, it displays the range of subtropical to temperate zone plants, fruits and herbs in Yakushima. Open: March - Aug 08.00 - 17.30 / Sept - Feb 08.00- 16.00. Price: Adults ¥500 / Student ¥800 / Child ¥250. Tel: 47-2636.

PONTANKAN (ポンタン館) is a great place to buy souvenirs and local produce both to eat and drink there or take back with you. It is on the mountain side of Route 77 just north of Tainokawa Bridge (鯛の川 橋). You can park here for Toroki-no-taki Waterfall as detailed below. Hours: 8:30 - 17:30. Closed on holidays. Tel: 47-2557.

TOROKI-NO-TAKI WATERFALL (トローキの滝)

• Just south of Mugio and before the large red bridge, there is a tiny path on the sea side of the road to view Toroki-no-taki. You can park opposite in the car park of the 'Pontankan' center (ポンタン館).

• Get off at No.87 Tainokawa (鯛ノ川) bus stop and look for the stone sign marking the path on the sea-side of the road.

There is not that much to see apart from the waterfall in the distance and you might have to crane your neck to see through the bushes but it is one of only two waterfalls in the whole of Japan to flow directly into the sea.

The height of the waterfall is an unspectacular 6 m but if you follow the path to the end, the mountain backdrop (Mochomu dake) and the bridge just behind make it all the more impressive a picture.

The 'Pontankan' (ポンタン館) building in the car park across the road has toilets and sells locally grown food and locally made souvenirs (as detailed above).

HARA (原) AREA

WHERE TO EAT/DRINK

¥ **DOUBUCHI** (どうぶち) is a cafe on the sea side of Route 77 just south of Hara village. Get off at No.91 Doubuchi-gawa (泥淵川) bus stop. They serve tea and coffee and a pleasant outside area to drink it. The inside resembles more an eccentric living room than a cafe. They also sell their own honey. Price: ~ ¥500. Hours: 10.00 – 18.00. Tel: 49-3480.

¥¥ **NOMADO CAFE** (ノマドカフェ) serve tea and coffee and cheap Thai style cuisine for lunch. Spot the sign between Hara and Onoaida on the mountain side of Route 77. Price: Lunch ~ ¥2,000. Hours: Sat – Tues 11.30 – 17.00. Tel: 47-2851. Web: http://nomado-cafe.seesaa.net

WHERE TO STAY

¥¥ IYASHI NO YADO TONTON (癒しの宿とんとん) has a spa offering body massage, reflexology and hand massage. Take the next left turn after the bridge over Toroki falls (coming from Anbo direction). The bus stop is close by, No.88 Hara Iriguchi (原入口). There are a total of 4 rooms all with free Wi-Fi, TV, fridge and air-conditioning. Price: ¥5,000 ~ pp/n room only. Web: ton-2.travel.coocan.jp Email: iyashi-tonton@ nifty.com. Tel: 49-3560. Book via any of the large hotel finder websites i.e. booking.com or travel.rakuten.co.jp.

WHAT TO DO

SENPIRO-NO-TAKI WATERFALL (千尋の滝)

• Follow the signs heading inland at Hara (原). There are several routes from the main road all leading to the same windy 3 km road. Midway it makes a tight right turn but continue past the ponkan orchards and keep climbing until you reach the car park and souvenir store.

• Get off at any one of 3 bus stops in or near Hara. Either get off at N.87 Tainokawa (鯛ノ川) bus stop and walk 300m across the bridge to the signed right turn; Or get off at No.88 Hara Iriguchi (原入口) and walk (Onoaida direction) until the park where you turn right; Or get off at No.89 Hara (原) and walk (Anbo direction) to the park where you turn left. Whichever stop you get off at it is 2.3 km to the waterfall and 1.5 km before the waterfall the road makes a sharp right turn.

Follow the 100 m path to a viewing area some distance from the 60 m high falls. From there you can see (weather permitting) the most impressive feature of the waterfall and that is the granite that it flows on.

It is one solid piece of granite rock measuring somewhere between 200 m x 400 m and as such is the largest single piece in Japan. Senpiro (千尋) gets its name from the measurement of the distance between your

hands if you stand with your arms outstretched. This measurement is called one hiro (一尋). The size of the granite was therefore described as the size of 1,000 people standing arms outstretched side by side, hence 'Senpiro' ('Sen' [千]= 1,000 and 'piro'[尋] = measurement).

You could once walk up to the waterfall but the path was closed due to the deaths of 3 hikers in a flash flood when trying to cross the river with their guide in 2003. The lookout point is usually busy with tourists as it is so accessible, but is worth seeing purely for that spectacularly large chunk of granite.

MOCHOMU DAKE TRAIL (M2) starts at the entrance of Senpiro-No-Taki Waterfall and is a 6.5 hour round trip up to the peak of Mt.Mochomu, the granite mountain which looms over the coast. As you walk from the carpark towards the waterfall, you will see the sign and the beginning of the trail on your left. If you are up to this tough hike, then check out the details in the M2 TRAIL section.

YAMANKO YUSUI SPRING WATER (山河湧水)

• On the mountain side of the main road in No.89 Hara (原), at the bridge midway through the village. Either side of the park there are side roads to stop in.

• Get off at No.89 Hara (原) bus stop and walk [Anbo direction] to the park on the mountain side of the main road.

This small park, Yamanko koen (山河公園), has picnic areas and a stream running through it. At the back of the park is bamboo piped spring water allowing you to fill up the bamboo cups provided with fresh cool mountain water from Mochomu dake.

ONOAIDA (尾之間) AREA

WHERE TO EAT/DRINK

¥ **PEITA** (ペイタ) is a bakery/cafe selling fresh bread, cakes and drinks. It is in the centre of Onoaida 200 m on the road leading to the JR Hotel. Price: ~ ¥1,000. Hours: 09.00-18.00. Closed Tues. Tel: 47-3166.

¥ **MOCHOMU VIEW TONE** (モッチョムビュートーン) serves set menus, noodles and curry in a relaxed atmosphere. The menu is in English with pictures. It is on the sea side of the Onoaida by-pass road, up the hill from the intersection to Onoaida Onsen with the gas station. Price: ~ ¥1,000. Hours: 11.00 – 20.30. Closed on Wed and 2nd & 4th

Thurs. Tel: 47-3775.

¥¥ **WARUNG KARANG** (ワルンカラン) is a Bali themed cafe serving 'Asian fusion' food. Turn towards the mountains at the Onoadia Onsen intersection on Route 77 (the gas station is on the other side) and climb towards Onoaida Onsen. Look for the small sign on your right and turn into the narrow road. Price: ~ ¥2,000.   Hours: Lunch 11:30 - 14:00; Dinner 18:00 - 21:00 (reservation the day before). Closed Wed and Thurs, and during winter season. Tel: 70-6927-8336. Web: http://warung-karang.com

WHERE TO STAY

¥¥ **CHINRYU-AN** (枕流庵) is a small, friendly guesthouse south of Onoaida, very used to foreigners and with English spoken. It is at No.101 Yaishi (矢石) bus stop heading out of Onoaida to Hirauchi. Price: ¥5,100 ~ pp/n including meals and ¥3,900 pp/n ~ without. Also offers rental gear and bicycles. Tel: 47-3900 Email: c@chinryu.com Web: chinryu.com (English). Book direct in English.

¥¥¥ **SHIKINOYADO ONOAIDA** (四季の宿尾之間) is just after the large red sign of the man in the Hawaiian shirt on Route 77, turn right (coming from Anbo direction). Very friendly and welcoming owner who speaks great English. Free Wi-Fi. Price: ¥8,500 ~. Tel: 47-3377. Web: h3.dion.ne.jp/~yasuakim/english.html (English)

¥¥¥¥ **JR HOTEL YAKUSHIMA** (ＪＲホテル屋久島) has panoramic sea/mountain views from its cliff-top location, its own onsen and the rooms have Wi-Fi. In the center of Onoaida and signed from the main road. Price: ¥13,000 ~ pp/n for a twin. Tel: 47-2011 Web: http://www.jrk-hotels.co.jp/en/Yakushima/ (English). You can also book via any of the large hotel finder websites i.e. booking.com or travel.rakuten.co.jp

¥¥¥¥ **YAKUSHIMA IWASAKI HOTEL** (屋久島いわさきホテル) is an impressive hotel with a tree growing in the lobby, its own waterfall path and its own shuttle bus. It can be seen rising out of the forest west of Onoaida and has its own turn off just outside of the village, heading towards Hirauchi. It boasts a swimming pool, gym and a hiking course from their gardens. Price: ¥22,000 ~ Tel: 47-3888 Web: http://yakushima.iwasakihotels.com/en/ (English). You can also book via any of the large hotel finder websites i.e. booking.com or travel.rakuten.co.jp

WHAT TO DO

¥ ONOAIDA ONSEN (尾之間温泉)
This authentic hot spring is at the start of the Onoaida Trail (O2)

and has a foot bath outside for tired hikers, should you not wish to reveal all. It is signed towards the mountains at the main intersection (the gas station is on the opposite corner) in Onoaida and is at the end of the side road after 500 m. By bus get off at No.98 Onoaida Onsen Entrance (尾之間温泉入口) bus stop and turn inland.

It was discovered as a hot spring 350 years ago, is run by a spectacularly unfriendly woman and the bath is rather basic - you need to bring everything with you (soap, towel, shampoo) and can also get busy as it is free to use for Onoaida residents. It is however natural and has piping hot (44-49°C) sulphur water. Hours: 07.00-21.00 Price: Adult: ¥200 Child: ¥100. Tel: 47-2872 (Closed Mon am)

ONOAIDA TRAIL (O2)

The O2 Trail starts at Onoaida Onsen and if you fancy a 3-4 hour reasonably-demanding roundtrip hike, you can follow the trail to Janokuchi Waterfall. For more details see the O2 Trail section.

¥¥ JR HOTEL YAKUSHIMA ONSEN (ＪＲホテル屋久島温泉)

This hot spring is in the JR Hotel on the clifftop in Onoaida with great views out to sea from the huge onsen windows. There is a small outdoor section and all equipment - towels, soap, and shampoo - is provided. Partly artificially heated alkaline water though and the temperature is low at 34.7°C. Hours: 15.00-18.00. Price: ¥1,400 ~ Tel: 47-2011 Web: http://www.jrk-hotels.co.jp/en/Yakushima/

¥¥ KAMI-NO-YU ONSEN (神の湯温泉)

This hot spring is inside Yakushima Iwasaki Hotel and offers nonguests use of their sulphur hot spring. Get off at No.100 Iwasaki Hotel Iriguchi bus stop. Hours: 15.00-22.00. Price: ¥1,300 ~ Web: http://yakushima.iwasakihotels.com/en

8 FOOD/ACCOMMODATION/SIGHTS
THE SOUTH WEST

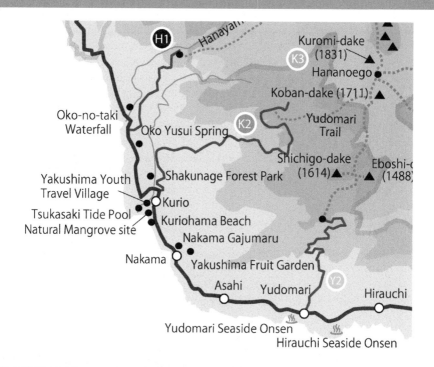

HIRAUCHI (平内) AREA

WHERE TO EAT/DRINK

¥ **NAA YUU CAFE** (なーゆーカフェ) serves drinks, snacks and simple set lunches in cosy surroundings. It is midway between Koshima and Hirauchi signed off Route 77 towards the sea. Price: ~ ¥1,000. Tel: 49-3195. Web: http://charu.air-nifty.com/naayuu/naa-yuu-cafe.html

¥¥ **HACHIMAN** (はちまん) serves seafood and a set menu during the day but also functions as a pub at night. Opposite the turning to Hachiman Elementary School (八幡小学校) on the main road in Hirauchi. If it is open, the sign will be hanging. Price: Lunch ~ ¥2,000. Hours: Open 11.30 – 14.00 & 18.00 – 23.00. Closed lunchtime Sat & Sun; Evenings Sun & Mon. Tel: 47-2888.

WHERE TO STAY

¥ **YAKUSHIMA SOUTH VILLAGE** (屋久島サウスビレッジ) is just north of Hirauchi village and is signed on the main road. By bus get off at No.107 Hirauchi Iriguchi (平内入口) bus stop. It offers dorms and rooms in the main youth hostel buildings as well as camping on raised wooden platforms. You can also rent hiking equipment, bicycles and cars. The setting is fairly isolated but Hirauchi Kaichu Onsen (平内海中温泉) is nearby and it is always busy. Open all year round. Price: ¥3-4,000 ~ pp/n (dorm or private room) with a minimum stay of 3 nights. Campsite is ¥1,000 ~ pp/n. Tel: 47-3751 Web: http://www.yakushima-yh. net/guesthouse_en.html (English) Email: yakushimasouth@gmail.com

¥¥¥ **GUESTHOUSE VIEWS** (ゲストハウスビューズ) is on the mountainside in Koshima. It is a rental home designed by an American architect who lives nearby to allow visitors to experience the forest around them. It has its own onsen-style bath with a private seated outdoor area, a large garden, kitchen and a tatami mat room with low windows so you can see outside when in bed. Attention to detail is impressive and everything is spotless. The owners live next door and speak English. Price: ¥20,000 ~ a night for 2 people. The longer you stay, the cheaper the price per night. Web: www13.plala.or.jp/views. Or contact them on facebook: www.facebook.com/yakushima.views. You can directly book in English through booking.com. Tel: 47-3234.

WHAT TO DO

HIRAUCHI KAICHU ONSEN (平内海中温泉)

• Turn towards the sea at the sign between Hirauchi and Yudomari. After 500 m there is a turning and a very small car park.

• Get off either at No.113 Nishikaikon (西開墾) or No.112 Hirauchi kaichu onsen (平内海中温泉) bus stops and head towards the sea for 500 m where the road curves around and there is the path to the onsen.

You need to choose your time to take this onsen as the sea can swallow it at high tide. The best time to come is an hour before or an hour after low tide. You can find the exact time with the app at www. yakumonkey.com/p/tides-in-yakushima. There is a strict rule that bathers have to leave their clothes a few meters from the bath which can be embarrassing depending on the audience. Ladies should come equipped with a thin white towel to wrap around. There tends to be a steady stream of people who come to see the bath so for modest bathers it may feel a little uncomfortable. The water is supposed to be good for rheumatism and neuralgia. Open 24 hours. Price: ¥100 (in a donation box).

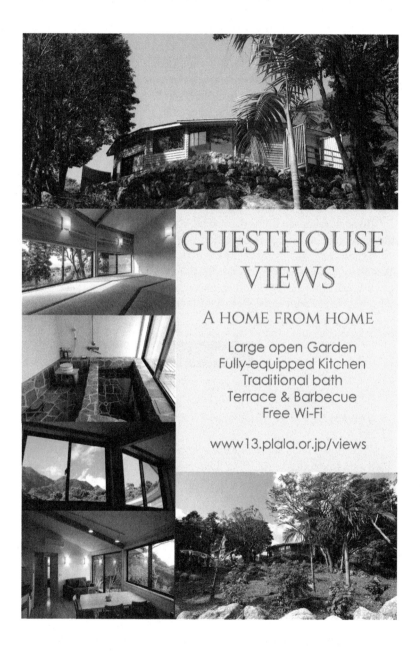

YUDOMARI (湯泊) AREA

WHAT TO DO

YUDOMARI SEASIDE ONSEN (湯泊温泉)

• Turn towards the sea at the sign on the main road in Yudomari village. After 200 m, turn left (the 3rd left) and then after another 200 m take a sharp left and the car park is in front.

• Get off at No.114 Yudomari (湯泊) bus stop and walk (Kurio direction) to the signed turning towards the sea. After 200 m, turn left (the 3rd left) and then after another 200 m take a sharp left and the entrance is ahead.

This natural onsen is less dependent of the tide than Hirauchi and the male and female section has a bamboo screen between. There are toilets and changing rooms at the car park. Of the two outdoor onsens, Yudomari is much better in its layout, although people will still come to gawk at you. There is also another even more private bath in the rocks if you follow the path at the side of the fence to the end. Open 24 hours. Price: ¥100 (in a donation box).

NAKAMA (中間) AREA

WHAT TO DO

NAKAMA BEACH (中間浜) and NAKAMA GAJYUMARU (中間ガジュマル)

• Nakama is 3 km south of Kurio. Both sides of the road here are lined with low concrete walls but there is a gravel parking area at the far end of the beach. There is also a small parking area near the Gajyumaru, 200 m inland from the main road.

• Get off at No.123 Nakama (中間) bus stop and the beach is in front. Walk for about 100 m (Kurio direction) and turn inland then follow the road through Nakama for 300 m to the Gajyumaru.

The beach is accessible through gaps in the sea wall. It is made up of coarse grained sand and often frequented by turtles in nesting season. The collection of Gajyumaru is worth a side trip if only to see how the vines weave an archway over the road.

¥ YAKUSHIMA FRUIT GARDEN (屋久島フルーツガーデン)

• Turn inland just east of Nakama River and take either the first or second right. The way is clearly signed.

• Get off at No.123 Nakama (中間) bus stop and walk back 200 m across the river. Take the first left and continue on next to the river, past Nakama Gajyumaru (中間ガジュマル) on your left across the bridge, and take the next right after that (about a 20 min walk).

Price: Adults ¥500 / Children ¥250. Around 1,600 types of tropical fruits and plants are grown here and you are guided around in a group (only in Japanese). At the end of the tour you also get to taste a selection of the seasonal fruit. Hours: 08.30-16.30. Tel: 48-2468.

KURIO (栗生) AREA

WHERE TO EAT/DRINK

¥¥ **SHOCHIKU** (松竹) is a traditional restaurant which offers handmade Soba noodles. Seating is on tatami mats. At the intersection before Kurio Bridge turn inland towards Kurio Elementary school (栗生小学校) and it is on your right. Look for the wooden lantern on the wall. Price: Lunch ~ ¥2,000. Hours: 11.00 – 15.00; 18.00 – 21.00. Tel: 48-2323. Web: http://sobaya-matutake.com/menu.htm

WHERE TO STAY

¥ **YAKUSHIMA YOUTH TRAVEL VILLAGE** (屋久島青少年旅行村) is on the west side of Kurio River. Cross the bridge and head up the hill towards Oko-no-taki. It has facilities for camping (showers/ toilets/ covered cooking area/washing machines) and a flat grass area for tents and also a section in the trees. Tents, cooking equipment, firewood and blankets can be rented. Price: ¥420 pp/n ~ for adults and ¥315 ~ per child (under 6). There are also 9 rental bungalows with aircon/kitchen priced at ¥12,600 ~ for 4 people. Close to Kurio beach and Tsukasaki Tide Pool. Open April 1st to Oct 31st. Tel: 48-2871.

WHAT TO DO

KURIO BEACH (栗生浜海水浴場)
• The car park is just as you reach Kurio (from Onoaida direction). On the left there is an old fishing boat perched beside a small cafe. Turn left straight after it.
• Get off at No.125 Kurio Iriguchi (栗生入口) bus stop and walk (Onoaida direction) for 1 min. It is on the right.
This is a small sandy beach at the mouth of Kurio River. It is bordered

either side by the concrete blocks of the harbour to prevent the beach being eroded. There is a concrete shelter at the top of the beach for shade and the changing rooms next to the toilets are open in July and August (09.00 - 18.00). It is a popular, safe beach for swimming and is frequented by turtles in hatching season.

NATURAL MANGROVE SITE (メヒルギ自生地区)

• Park before Kurio Bridge (on the opposite side to Kurio village) at the side of the main road. Then follow the track that runs beside the river towards the sea.

• Get off at No.127 Kurio bashi (栗生橋) bus stop. Take the track by the river heading towards the sea. At the end of the track follow the path to a stone sign and the mangroves are ahead.

This site is recognised as an example of the rare distribution of the mangrove tree species. Mangroves are common in the southern islands of the Ryukyu chain but not normally found at this latitude. The trees themselves have rooted on the riverside sandbank and bloom from late summer with a white 5 petalled flower.

¥ SHAKUNAGE FOREST PARK (石楠花の森公園)

• Turn right after Kurio Bridge at the sign and take the single track road through small landholdings to the end where there is a car park.

• Get off at No.127 Kurio bashi (栗生橋) bus stop and walk inland on the single track road.

'Shakunage' means 'rhododendron' and the best time to visit here is in the rhododendron flowering season which is from April to June. The trail leads on a wooden walkway beside Kurio River and then opens out into a large garden brimmed full with rhododendrons and with access to the river. It is very beautiful around the crystal clear river and both sides are bordered by thick forest. Hours: April to Aug: 09.00-18.30/Sept to March: 09.00-16.00. Price: Adults ¥500 / Child ¥250.

TSUKASAKI TIDE POOL (塚崎タイドプール)

• Go across Kurio Bridge and continue up the hill towards Oko-no-taki waterfall. It is signed to the left on the bend. Go through Yakushima Youth Travel village (屋久島青少年旅行村) and at the end, take the single track road to the left which runs beside the mouth of Kurio River. At the end of that there is a small car park in front of a picnic shelter and a basic shower block.

• Get off at No.128 Seishonen-mura (青少年村) bus stop and walk down through Yakushima Youth Travel village.

Tsukasaki Tide Pool is a safe place to go snorkeling. You can find the tide times with the app at www.yakumonkey.com/p/tides-in-yakushima. It is best between high and low tide. At low tide it is still possible to snor-

kel but it is at its best when relatively full with water as the fish are so plentiful. The pool is at the river mouth and bordered by rocks apart from the opening in the far left corner closest to the sea. The closer you snorkel to here, the more fish there should be. Watch out for the colourful trigger fish which, despite their small size, may nip at you. Its position at the mouth of Kurio River means that visibility can sometimes be affected as the fresh and salt water mix.

OKO YUSUI MOUNTAIN SPRING WATER (大川湧水)

Shortly before Oko-no-taki waterfall there is a lay-by on the mountain side of the main road. Stop here and you will see a wooden sign and a small spring. The water is drinkable and straight from the mountain river.

OKO-NO-TAKI WATERFALL (大川の滝)

• Signed inland at a bend on the main road, 4 km north of Kurio. A single lane track leads you 200 m across a small concrete bridge and there is a very small car park immediately to the left. If necessary park at a safe place on the roadside going up under the large bridge.

• Get off at No.129 Oko-no-taki (大川の滝) bus stop (the final destination) and it is a 300 m walk to the waterfall. The bus stop is close to Oko spring water above.

The size and volume of water of this 88m high waterfall makes it the largest in Yakushima and the highest in southern Kyushu. It has been selected as one of 'the best 100 waterfalls in Japan' and the water pool in front of the waterfall, one of the 'best 100 bodies of water in Japan'.

There is a concrete walkway by the side of the river which ends at a concrete picnic table and from then on clamber over the rocks for a closer look. If you arrive around 3 pm a rainbow is sometimes visible in the spray.

In times of low rainfall the water trickles down gently but in the rainy season the valley is a raging torrent. The whole 20m-wide rock face gushes water, smothering the concrete pathway and picnic table completely and threatening to reach the height of the bridge. When the river is seen at its fiercest you can understand how the gi-ant boulders that stand in the valley were originally brought there.

The river continues on for around 500m to the sea and is accessible via a path leading down to a small toilet block. Continue along the stony track and you will arrive after 5 min at Sagoshi-no-hama (サゴシの浜), a secluded bay at the mouth of the river.

9 FOOD/ACCOMMODATION/SIGHTS
THE NORTH WEST

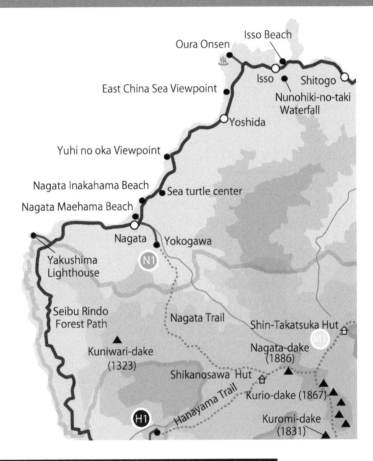

SEIBU RINDO FOREST PATH (西部林道)

WHAT TO DO

On the west side of the island the World Heritage Site Protection Area extends all the way down to the seashore and the Seibu Rindo road cuts its way through this thick forest between Nagata and Kurio. From both directions the road rises steeply with plenty of blind forested bends

APOLLO RESORT MARINE BLUE YAKUSHIMA

Located directly on the white sands of Nagata Inakahama beach. Rooms include a sofa and private bathroom, and open directly onto a wide terrace overlooking the sea. Perfect for turtle-watching and relaxing in our sea-view onsen bath.

Reservations: http://travel.rakuten.com/hotel/info/49401/

and continues like this for a windy 26½ km until the descent down to the coast.

As the single track road rises towards Kuniwari dake (国割岳) there are many scenic vantage points of the forest allowing you to see how the distribution of trees clearly changes both in colour and shape with altitude. It also is very common to spot troops of macaques and deer on or beside the road.

No buses run this route so options are limited without a car or motorbike, but with a little planning it is perfectly feasible by bicycle or on foot. There are plans to expand the road to make a complete circular road around the island which of course will have a major impact on the fragile environment that exists here if followed through.

NAGATA (永田) AREA

WHERE TO EAT/DRINK

¥¥ JYARAITEI (じゃらい亭) serves traditional Yakushima dishes like black pork cutlets (黒豚カツ) and flying fish (トビウオ) as well as more typical Japanese food. From No.2 Nagata Iriguchi (永田入口) bus stop head towards the mountains and look for the sign. Price: Lunch ~ ¥2,000. Hours: 11.00-14.00 (Oct-April) & 18.00-23.00. Closed Mon. Tel: 45-2078.

WHERE TO STAY

¥¥¥ APOLLO RESORT MARINE BLUE YAKUSHIMA (アポロリゾート マリンブルー屋久島) is the only hotel which actually positioned on Nagata Inagahama beach (永田いなか浜). Rooms are all facing a wide decking area which leads directly to the beach and facing the sea. Rooms are fairly standard but that is not why people stay here. They stay for the stunning views and sunsets. Price: ¥9,700 ~ pp/n with two meals. Book via any of the large hotel finder websites i.e. booking.com or travel.rakuten.co.jp

¥¥ MINSHUKU INAKAHAMA (民宿いなか浜) has 4 immaculate tatami rooms across the road from the south end of Inakahama beach. Rooms have an en-suite toilet but the modern bath is shared. No reservations are required to participate in the turtle events in the summer (see the turtle egg laying/hatching sections below). Price: ¥8,400 ~ pp/n with 2 meals. TEL & FAX: 45-2233. Book in English via travel.rakuten.co.jp.

¥¥¥¥ **SOYOUTEI**（送陽邸）is a beautiful set of traditional build-ings sat the far end of Inagahama beach. It is a hotel with a very exclusive feel to it and you can eat and take a private bath directly overlooking the sea. There is also a private covered hammock area to swing away your stresses. Often featured in glossy magazines about Yakushima. No reservations are required to participate in the turtle events in the sum-mer (see the turtle egg laying/hatching sections below). Price: ¥12,900 ~ pp/n. Web: www.soyotei.net. Book direct. TEL + FAX: 45-2819. Also see TURTLE EGG LAYING section below

WHAT TO DO

YAKUSHIMA LIGHTHOUSE (屋久島灯台)
• Yakushima lighthouse is at Nagatamisaki (永田岬), on the edge of the Seibu Rindo path and is signed 5 km west of Nagata. Take the side road for 1 km until the car park at the end.

There has been a lighthouse here since 1897 to protect the main ship routes in the deep waters to the north west of the island. The actual lighthouse itself is nothing special but there are beautiful views of Kuchinoerabu (口永良部島) island and other more distant islands from the cliff top. It is also a good place to see the blooming pink flower of the Marubasatsuki or Azalea plants in early summer.

NAGATA RIVER (永田川) and YOKKO VALLY (横河渓谷)
• Turn inland just before Nagata Bridge (永田橋) at the gas station and keep parallel to the river. This may mean taking a left turn depending on which way you came from. Continue parallel to the river for 1 km to the small bridge to the left (do not cross it) and follow the road up for a further 300 m. There will be an old weathered sign and a small turning to the left into the Nagata Trail car park.
• Get off at No.1 Nagata (永田) bus stop and walk inland parallel to the river. After 1 km a bridge crosses the river to your left, do not cross it but continue for a further 300 m to the car park of the trail. (30 min walk).

From the beginning of the Nagata Trail (N1) (永田歩道) follow the paved path until it becomes forest floor and carefully hop over a stream. After 6 min there is a naturally formed swimming area complete with a slippery rock waterslide on your left. This is known as YOKOGAWA or locally as YOKKO VAL-LEY (横河渓谷). You get a few glimpses of it through the trees before you reach the collection of rocks that lead you down to the

river. In the summer months it is a popular spot for a picnic or to take a dip in the crystal clear water. On a safety note, visit here with caution after heavy rains as like many of Yakushima's rivers, it is prone to flash floods.

NAGATA INAKAHAMA BEACH (永田いなか浜)

• Less than 1 km north of Nagata village. Park in any of the gravel lay-bys next to the beach.

• Get off at No.4 Inakahama (いなか浜) bus stop.

This is the longest stretch of sandy beach on the island. From May to July it is the focal point of loggerhead turtle egg laying activity and nesting areas are usually roped off with bamboo posts and signs. Care should be taken not to climb over any barriers erected as these are to protect newly laid legs from being trampled. At sundown the beach is patrolled by volunteers monitoring the turtles. Outside of this time however there are no restrictions and the beach is a welcome relief from the forest all around.

¥ SEA TURTLE CENTER (うみがめ館)

• On the mountain side of the road, mid-way along Inakahama beach (いなか浜) in Nagata. Park in the beach-side car park.

• Get off at No.5 Nakanobashi (中野橋) bus stop and walk 200 m (Nagata village direction) or get off at No.4 Inakahama (いなか浜) bus stop and walk 200 m (Isso direction). The centre is across the street from the beach. Price: Adults ¥300 / Students ¥100. Closed on Tuesdays.

This is run by the YAKUSHIMA UMIGAME CENTRE (屋久島うみがめ館), a Non-Profit Organisation (NPO) set up to protect the sea turtles on Nagata's beaches. The center has shells, models, pictures and maps of turtle activity around Yakushima and information on some of the exhibits is in both Japanese and English. Open all year (Closed on Tuesdays) 09.00-17.00. During the nesting and hatching seasons it opens at night. Tel: 49-6550. Web: http://www.k4.dion.ne.jp/~umigame/top_english.html

There are two important events that take place every year here and

if you are lucky enough to be in Yakushima at these times, you get the chance to see the turtles in action:

¥¥ TURTLE EGG LAYING

This is run by the Nagata Sea Turtle Liaison Council (永田ウミガメ連絡協議会) which has recently taken over responsibility of the turtles.

This is a division of the Ministry of the Environment and has wrested control over the turtles from the local volunteer NPO which had up until recently been solely responsible. From mid-May to the end of July, Inakahama beach becomes a hive of activity at night. The focal point is in the collection of huts just in front of the beach, a short distance from the turtle centre. Open May 1st to Aug 31st 19.30-21.00. Price for adults: ¥1,500 (¥500 of this is a donation to the Yakushima Umigame Centre NPO). Tel: 090-8768-4281 FAX: 45-2484. Web: www.nagata-umigame.com

The number of visitors has been restricted per night so you need to reserve your place in advance in order not to be turned away. This can be done though your accommodation, directly or through the tourist information offices.

If you are staying in the following accommodation in Nagata, you do not need any reservations. Even if full, you will still be able to participate in egg laying watching:

¥¥ MINSHUKU INAKAHAMA (listed earlier)

¥¥¥¥ SOYOTEI (送陽邸) (listed earlier)

¥¥¥ MINSHUKU EBISU (民宿ゑびす) Tel: 45-2156. ¥9,000 ~ pp/n. Web: www.ac.auone-net.jp/~ebisum/index.html (Japanese).

¥¥ MINSHUKU YAMACHON (民宿やまちょん) Tel: 45-2832. ¥6,500 ~ pp/n. No Web.

¥¥ MAKI RYOKAN (牧旅館) Tel: 45-2006. ¥8,400 ~ pp/n. Web: http://www.geocities.jp/makiryokan (Japanese).

¥¥¥ YAKU-NO-KO HOUSE (屋久の子の家) Tel: 45-2137. ¥9,800 ~ pp/n. Web: http://yakunoko.jp Email: info@yakunoko.jp

¥¥ MINSHUKU NAGATADAKE (民宿ながた岳) Tel: 45-2304. ¥7,500 ~ pp/n. Web: www.nagatadake.com (Japanese).

Pay in the admin hut and then wait for the first part of the evening which is a lecture on turtles. There are 3 sessions for this, the first starting at 19.30, the next at 20.00 and the last at 20.30 with up to 40 people in each time slot.

After that you have to wait. The turtles could come at any time so the wait could be long or short and there are some nights when no turtle comes at all. Whatever happens it all comes to an end at 23.00.

If you are lucky it will be a short wait before one is spotted laying eggs and you are told to follow one of the guides. This could be right in front of the hut on the beach or it could be 1 km away on one of the other beaches.

When you reach the egg laying turtle, the guide will shine a torch and explain (in Japanese) about the process. It takes around an hour before the turtle is finished and flips sand back into the hole to seal it. It will then drag itself back into the sea and the show ends.

It is forbidden to take photos with a flash and to get too close while with the turtle for obvious reasons.

¥¥ HATCHING OF BABY TURTLES

Again this is now run by the Nagata Sea Turtle Liaison Council (永田ウミガメ連絡協議会) and happens August 1st to August 31st from 19.30 to 21.30. The visitors are organised into 3 groups with staggered times and begins with a lecture about the turtles in the turtle centre (in Japanese) and then a trip across the road to the beach where staff will release baby turtles and you can observe them struggle along the beach to the sea. Price for adults: ¥1,500 (¥500 of this is a donation to the Yakushima Umigame Centre NPO).

These baby turtles are hatched from eggs collected by the centre from vulnerable parts of the beach in the egg laying season a few months before. They are no longer at risk of being dug up for food – the consumption of turtle eggs was banned in Yakushima in 1973 and then later in 1988 in Kagoshima Prefecture. But they are at risk of being trampled underfoot or being eaten by scavengers like the recently introduced raccoon dog.

ISSO (一湊) AREA

WHERE TO STAY

¥ **ISSO OURA CAMPSITE** (大浦キャンプ場) is right next to Oura onsen in a remote, secluded bay facing the sea. From Miyanoura direction continue past Isso and as the road becomes steeper turn right at the sign for the onsen （大浦温泉）. By bus get off at No.10 Oura (大浦) bus stop. Follow the road right to the end and the campsite is on the right of the tiny onsen. Pay in the onsen office. Price: Camping is ¥700 (¥400 for tent and ¥300  for person) p/n. So for 2 people it costs ¥1,000 p/n. Check in: 9.00-19.00. Check out: 9.00-19.00. Tel: 44-2800. Web: www.isso-yakushima.com/oouracamp.html.

WHAT TO DO

¥ OURA ONSEN (大浦の湯)

This is the Onsen mentioned above which is next to Isso Oura Campsite. It is very small and basic but right next to the beach. The paint is coming off, everything is faded and it appears to be from another age. For some this might be turn-off but for others a memorable experience. They don't come more traditional than this! Hours: 11.00 to 19.00 Price: ¥300. Tel: 44-2800.

NUNOHIKI-NO-TAKI WATERFALL (布引の滝)

This has a car park, immaculate toilets and rest area and is on the main by-pass road at Isso, 200 m from Isso Bridge. The closest bus stop is No.12 Isso Iriguchi (一湊入口). The water is little more than a trickle unless after heavy rain when it becomes a torrent.

ISSO BEACH (一湊海水浴場)

• Signed just East of Isso Route 78. Look for the car park.
• Get off at No.13 Yahazu (矢筈) bus stop which is close to the car park.

A large triangular picnic shelter and a concrete frame of a building lead on to a steep sandy beach. In the summer months it is one of the most popular swimming sites with beach/swim equipment for rent and refreshments in temporary huts.

There are concrete blocks laid on the sea bed 200 m out which reduces wave impact on the beach. The shower blocks open in July and August (09.00 - 18.00).

From the beach you may be able to see a red Torii (鳥居) gate on the right headland. This marks the entrance to Isso Yahazudake Shrine (一湊矢筈嶽神社) and the access road is the side road which runs east of the main road behind the car park. The sign says Yahazu Park (矢筈公園) and if you take the left fork, it will take you to the start of the path marked by another red gate. A local story tells of a cat which got lost in this cave while chasing a mouse, only to reappear some time later in Kumano shrine in Tanegashima Island. Unfortunately path has been in disrepair for some time and has been blocked.

If you take the road to the end of the headland, however, there is a car park and the remains of Yahazu Park's recreational area which has now overgrown but there is still a footpath to the cliffs with views out to sea.

10 TRAIL HIKING

Hiking on Yakushima covers some of the best walking trails in Japan and are highly rated from casual walkers to serious climbers. There are several trails leading from the coast which are usually more demanding but there are also trails which start further into the inland mountains and even the most challenged walker can find a suitable path to enjoy the forest.

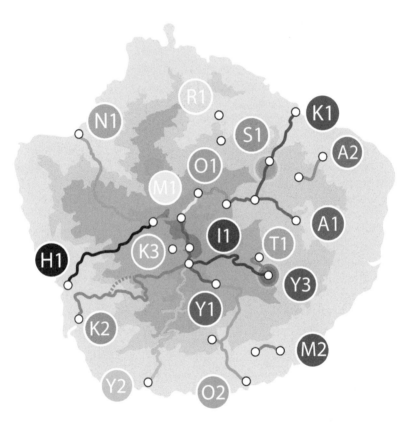

HALF DAY HIKES

LIGHT HIKING

If hiking is not really your thing but you would like to see some of the forest and the old Yakusugi trees, try the following hikes:

- Yakusugiland (Y3) is ideal and gives a choice of trails from sturdy wooden platforms to scrambling on all fours.
- Shiratani Unsuikyo (S1) also offers a variety of trails and the chance to see one of the mountain huts.

Even if hiking is your thing, however, both of these trails above offer something for everyone and you get a real sense of Yakushima, especially on the longer courses.

MEDIUM HIKING

- The Onoaida Trail (O2) to Janokuchi Waterfall from Onoaida Onsen, is on the coast which can be a good choice if cloud is covering the mountains, although even here there are a few steep sections. The real bonus of this trail is that when you come back, you are right outside Onoaida Onsen which also has a foot bath for your sore feet.
- The Yodogawa Trail (Y1) but only as far as the sweeping views of the high mountains from the top of Kuroimi dake (K3).
- The Tachu dake Trail (T1) from Yakusugiland offers views across the whole eastern part of the island.
- The Ryujinsugi Trail (R1) from Miyanoura leads through thick forest to rarely visited Yakusugi.

STRENUOUS HIKING

If you want to hike up steep trails which include ropes, ladders and stunning views over the coast.

- The Aiko dake Trail (A2) from Koseda is a steep climb but offers panoramic 360° views from its peak.
- The Mochomu dake Trail (M2) from near Hara offers a dramatic view of the granite mountains and the Southern coastline.

FULL DAY HIKES

Most people who visit Yakushima want to see 2 things:

• **JOMON SUGI** via the Arakawa Trail (A1) and Okabu Trail (O1) for a 9 to 12-hour round trip.

• **JOMON SUGI** via the Kusugawa Trail (K1), Arakawa Trail (A1) and the Okabu Trail (O1) for a 9 to 12-hour round trip.

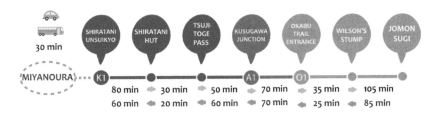

• **MIYANOURA DAKE**, the highest mountain in Southern Japan, via the Yodogawa Trail (Y1) for a 9 to 10-hour day trip.

2+ DAY HIKES

Many hikers combine the trails and cross the island, spending the night in some of the 6 mountains huts. Here are common trail combinations:

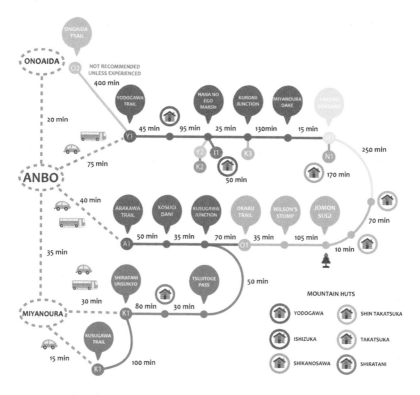

Note that the Onoaida Trail (O2) has been flagged as not recommended as a hike combination. This is due to the pleading of the Tourism Department who have expressed concerns of the number of unprepared hikers taking this route. They want to make it clear that the Onoaida Trail becomes very dangerous the higher it gets especially with river crossings after heavy rain. Unless you are experienced and well-prepared, it might be best to start your hike higher up.

There are a selection of other trails such as the Nagata trail (N1), Yodogawa trail (Y2), Kurio trail (K2), Onoaida trail (O2), Yudomari trail (Y2) and the Hanayama trail (H1) all of which offer another level of hiking and with the right equipment, preparation and state of mind, offers the serious hiker a real challenge.

HIKING EQUIPMENT

To enjoy your time safely on any of the mountain trails, it is highly recommended that you have at least the following equipment:
- Hiking boots
- Water-proof rain gear
- Hiking map
- Compass
- Flashlight and spare batteries
- Basic food provisions (enough for your journey)
- Water container
- Towel
- Gloves
- Long-sleeved shirt
- Toilet paper
- Backpack

Of course if you intend to stay in the huts, you will need a lot more. Including cooking equipment and a sleeping bag and outside of the summer you will need extra clothes to keep warm. A mobile is also a useful addition as at various points in the mountains, reception is good enough to make a call (from the top of Miyanoura dake, Nagata dake and the surrounding peaks, at some points on the trail to Jomon Sugi and the general rule of thumb - anywhere where you can see Tanegashima island).

A good hiking map to buy is the 'Yakushima/Miyanoura dake' map from the 'Yama-to-kogen chizu' series (山と高原地図屋久島宮之浦岳). It can be bought widely in Japan and online and is also available in Yakushima. There are no English translations but if used with this guide or a tourist map, it is very easy to follow.

If you arrived without much of the above but would like to take a mountain trail you are in luck because just about anything related to the mountains can be rented or bought in several stores on Yakushima.

Miyanoura area

• **NAKAGAWA SPORTS** (ナカガワスポーツ) has been in business for many years and is on the main street in Miyanoura. They sell and rent all kinds of mountain gear from rain wear, hiking boots and backpacks to dried food and repellent. They have limited English but are friendly, welcome foreigners and will help you out if they can. Hours: 9.00-19.00. Closed on Wed. Tel: 42-0341 Web: yakushima-sp.com.

• **YAKUSHIMA KANKO CENTER** (屋久島観光センター) is a large store near the entrance of Miyanoura port. They sell and rent a wide variety of mountain gear and marine sports equipment. They have limited English but this is the main tourist rental store so they have lots of experience. Hours: 8.00 - 21.00 Tel: 42-0091 Web: yksm.com.

Anbo area

• **MORI-NO-KIRAMEKI** (森のきらめき) is near the police station in Anbo. They sell and rent a wide variety of mountain gear. You can also register your mountain trip here. Hours: 07.30 - 19.00 Tel: 49-7101 Web: morinokirameki.com

Hirauchi area

• **YAKUSHIMA SOUTH VILLAGE** (屋久島サウスビレッジ) also rents hiking gear and waterproofs. Tel: 47-3751 Web: yakushima-yh.net

SAFE HIKING

The trails are generally safe and easy to follow but can be slippery and treacherous sometimes even on the most widely used trails.
Like all mountainous areas, be aware that accidents do happen and fatalities do occur. All the paths should be clearly marked with small pink ribbons tied to trees and the popular routes to Jomon Sugi and Miyanoura have wooden steps and walkways. It is however still possible to get lost especially when the weather deteriorates and care needs to be taken not to mistakenly follow a deer trail.

If you hike outside of an organised group it is suggested that you fill in a climbing form called a 'TOZAN TODOKE' (登山届け). This is a form (in Japanese or in English if you're lucky) in which you are supposed to detail your route and destination. To fill it in simply put your details, the address where you are 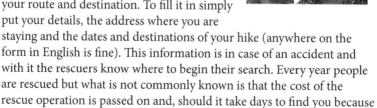 staying and the dates and destinations of your hike (anywhere on the form in English is fine). This information is in case of an accident and with it the rescuers know where to begin their search. Every year people are rescued but what is not commonly known is that the cost of the rescue operation is passed on and, should it take days to find you because your route is unknown, it will be your wallet and not only your body that is damaged.

These forms can usually be found at the trail entrance of the main trails where there is usually a wooden box to post your form. They can also be found at the airport, tourist information, police station, town hall and port. They are also available in English as a PDF file on **yakumonkey.com**.

MOUNTAIN RULES

There are few specific mountain rules for hiking in Yakushima - general common sense rules apply e.g. when encountering hikers, those ascending have priority (and etiquette dictates that you are expected to greet each and every hiker who passes). Due to the environmental impact of visitors, a set of hiking rules are promoted by Yakushima authorities.

1. Use the toilets provided.
2. Use the huts for accommodation and only camp in designated areas.
3. Keep to the trail. Follow the pink ribbon markers and be careful not to stray onto deer paths by mistake.
4. If lost, do not descend directly down a valley or follow the path of a river. There are many straight drops and waterfalls which may be hidden by the undergrowth.
5. Do not feed the animals.
6. Do not remove anything from its natural environment.
7. Bring your garbage back with you.
8. Keep the fresh water clean.

If you stay in the huts, this means not washing your cooking equipment in the nearby stream. Everything should be wiped with a damp cloth or tissue and disposed of later off the mountains.

THE DISPOSABLE TOILET KIT

 One of the solutions that have been successfully implemented to combat increasing numbers of hikers and the pollution that this can cause are the disposable toilet kits. These can be used in wooden cabins along the trails with a seat to which you are supposed to attach a toilet kit.

This covers the seat and keeps any contents safely sealed until you reach a disposal unit at the trail entrance. The toilet kit is small enough to fit in any small backpack and can be bought from a variety of places on Yakushima. One costs ¥400 and two ¥500.

MOUNTAIN HIKING GUIDES

There are many registered guides offering their services on Yakushima (but mostly in Japanese) and some tourists hire them for their hiking trips into the mountains. The benefit of having a guide is local knowledge of the flora and fauna, the trails and some security should there be a problem. For most people, provided they use common sense and have a basic awareness of what hiking in mountains involves, a guide really is not necessary as the trails are very well marked and in generally good condition.

If you still feel that you need one, there is a regulatory body called the Yakushima Guide Association (屋久島ガイド協会) Tel: 49-4191 Web: yakushima-guide.com and be careful to check that any potential guide is a member of this organisation as all members have adequate training and support. For a guide in English, try Cameron at yakushimaexperience.com.

MOUNTAIN HUTS

There are a total of 6 mountain huts on Yakushima. All of them offer a dry place to sleep, water from a stream and a toilet but little else, so all equipment for sleeping and cooking have to be carried with you. Depending on the time you visit you could be all alone or there may be a guided group of noisy, snoring tourists.

The huts are at the forefront of the environmental problems faced by the huge numbers of tourists who hike the paths in Yakushima. In high season many of the huts get very busy and it is not uncommon for them to be full, leaving no choice for some but to camp in the restricted area. So if you are planning to visit during busy times, bring a light tent. The toilets also are used beyond their capacity and have begun to pollute the surrounding area. If you stay in the huts be aware of the problems and try not to add to them. Remember, Yakushima is a World Heritage site and wild camping and camp fires are forbidden.

SHIRATANI HUT (白谷小屋)

Sleeps: 40
Material: Reinforced Concrete
Constructed: 1979
Altitude: 825 m
This hut is 2.1 km (1 hour 20 min) from Shiratani Unsuikyo (S1) car park which makes it a popular hut to start

from. The toilets are actually inside which, especially in summer, can cause odour problems. It has a wooden communal area to prepare food and also has three rooms with wooden slats to sleep on. Like all the huts it is first come, first served and if the rooms are full, find a place in the communal area. The Shiratani River flows right past the hut.

YODOGAWA HUT (淀川小屋)

Sleeps: 60
Material: Wood
Constructed: 1988
Altitude: 1380 m

Yodogawa Hut can be reached via Anbo on the Yakusugiland/Kigensugi Mountain Road and is a 45 min hike (1.5 km) from the Yodogawa Trail Entrance. As it is near the start of the Yodogawa Trail (Y1) and relatively easy to get to, it can be a very popular hut to stay in. In high season it can get crowded with hikers who take the road up in the late afternoon and begin their hiking to Miyanoura dake the following morning. Water can be found behind the hut where the Arakawa River passes by.

TAKATSUKA HUT (高塚小屋)

Sleeps: 20
Material: Strengthened cardboard
Constructed: 2013
Altitude: 1330 m

This small hut along the Okabu Trail (O1) is only a 10 min walk (200 m) from Jomon Sugi and consequently can get very busy. Water is piped and flows nearby. There are split level wooden racks to sleep on and there is a separate toilet hut. A wooden platform are is also provided for tents for when the hut is full.

SHIN-TAKATSUKA HUT (新高塚小屋)

Sleeps: 60
Material: Concrete/Wood
Constructed: 1992
Altitude: 1460 m

This hut is 1 km further up the Okabu Trail (O1) and is a hike of just over 1 hour from Takat-suka Hut. The sleeping is split level with ladders up to the higher wooden platform. There is an open space in front of the hut for cooking, piped fresh water from the river and a separate toilet nearby. From this hut upwards the Miyanoura Trail (M1) begins.

SHIKANO-SAWA HUT (鹿之沢小屋)

Sleeps: 20
Building structure: Stone
Constructed: 1965
Altitude: 1550 m

On the Nagata Trail (N1) 1.2 km from the summit of Nagata dake. The toilet is in a separate hut 50 m down the Nagata trail across the stream where drinking water is available. Sleeping is split level. The Nagata trail is long and arduous, the Hanayama trail is not popular and few people climb Nagata dake after climbing Miyanoura dake, so the hut is usually quite empty.

ISHIZUKA HUT (石塚小屋)

Sleeps: 20
Material: Concrete-blocks
Constructed: 1971
Altitude: 1600 m

This is 1.2 km (50 min) down the Ishizuka Trail (I1) from Hana-no-ego Marsh or 7.2 km (6 hours) up on the same trail from Yakusugiland. The toilet hut is a few meters away and water is from a stream 5 min along the path to Hana-no-ego. According to local people the hut is supposed to be haunted with the ghosts of an American bomber crew who crashed near Hana-no-ego Marsh during the Second World War.

SHELTERS

As an alternative to the huts if the weather closes in when around the high peaks, there are several cave like rock formations which provide shelter and some of them have plastic sheeting and other equipment stored for emergencies. For example, Hiraishi Iwaya (平石岩屋) on the Yodogawa Trail (Y1) up to Miyanoura can sleep up to 8 people in an emergency.

ARAKAWA TRAIL 荒川歩道

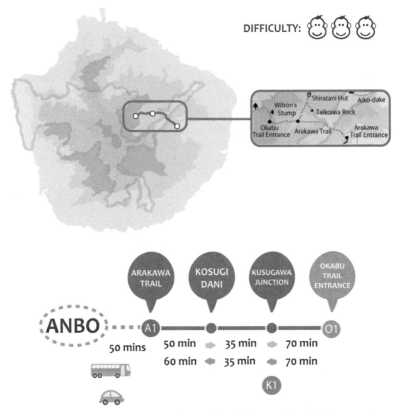

DIFFICULTY:

CAR/BUS: In order to protect the trail and the road that leads to it, private cars are prohibited from driving to the trail entrance. Instead several shuttle buses leave Yakusugi Museum car park and relay hikers to the start of the trail. Taxis and private tours can also drive up to the entrance but only with a pre-bought access ticket for every hiker. More details on this is in the Bus section.

The Arakawa Trail is by far the busiest trail in Yakushima as it leads on to the great Jomon Sugi, the goal of most visitors to Yakushima.

Most hikers depart along the trail early in the morning and in noisy guided groups. You can avoid these groups for much of the trail if you

Okabu Trail
Entrance

O1

Railroad

3.7 km

Sandai
sugi

Kusugawa
Junction

K1

Kusugawa
Trail

1.8 km

Bio-toilet

Kosugidani
bridge

Kosugidani

2.6 km

Railroad

Arakawa Trail
Entrance

A1

leave slightly later on but you will inevitably meet them somewhere along the route. Hiking out of season is the only way to avoid this.

The A1 Trail begins at a mountain sub-station of the logging railway which despite appearances is still very much in use. Until you reach the beginning of the Okabu Trail (O1) (大株歩道), the trail consists solely of walking on these rail road tracks (for a painful 9.1 km). Start by crossing the suspension bridge, go through the short tunnel which illuminates automatically as you pass through and from the rusty old engine on the right it is a 50 min walk (2.6 km) to **Kosugidani village** (小杉谷集落跡). Signs inform you periodically of 'rest' places to shelter from the train and be aware of them as you may have to jump out of the way of rumbling wagons coming towards you.

Just before Kosugidani, the track separates (careful not to continue on the branch straight on) and veers sharply right to Kosugidani Bridge (小杉谷橋). Anbo River below ranges from a gentle trickle to a raging torrent and signs of its power lie in the huge boulders dragged down the mountain dotted along the river bed.

Once you have crossed the bridge, you are in Kosugidani (小杉谷) and the rail track turns left continuing on the opposite bank. Be careful however not to miss the remains of this once vibrant logging village. There are displays of the large logging community that once made this place their home until the logging office was closed in 1970. At its height there were around 600 inhabitants, over 100 of them being children. The old elementary school to the right just after you cross the bridge allows you access to the river. It is reputed to be haunted here so take that into account if you linger after dark. There is also a shelter with more displays, a bio-toilet and piped drinking water to fill up any containers you have.

The path follows the old railway track for what will feel like an eternity from now on. It has a slight uphill gradient and meanders around the mountain slopes, crossing two smaller bridges. On the way there are a few landmarks to break up the monotony. The Kusugawa Trail (K1) leading from Shiratani meets the railway after 1.8 km at **Kusugawa Junction** (楠川分かれ) and there is a clearly marked sign informing you of the fork in the trail.

It is tempting on the way back to take this route as you tire of the railroad, but be aware that the trail is uphill for 1 hour from here and quite steep in places.

A short while after this (2 km after Kosugidani) you come across the first of the grand Yakusugis: **Sandaisugi** (三代杉) or 'Third Generation Cedar'. This is so called because when the original cedar fell, which was estimated at 1,200 years old, a second cedar grew on its remains. This then grew to be over 1,000 years old before being cut down by loggers, whereupon a third then perched itself on top and is currently around 350 years old. The tree stands at 38.4 m and is well worth a stop as you can see clearly how the generations have grown over one another with roots like tentacles grasping the ground.

 Just as you start cursing taking this uncomfortably uneven path and after a further 3.7 km of pounding the railway slats, it abruptly ends at the **Okabu Trail Entrance** (O1) (大株歩道入口).

O1 OKABU TRAIL
M1 MIYANOURA TRAIL

大株歩道
宮之浦歩道

DIFFICULTY: 😊 😊 😊

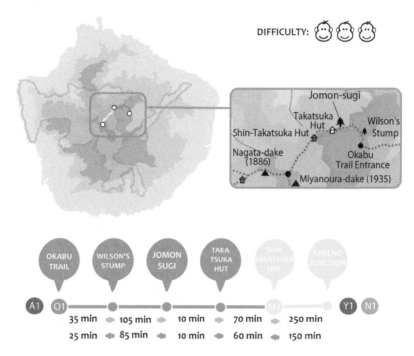

OKABU TRAIL	WILSON'S STUMP	JOMON SUGI	TAKA-TSUKA HUT	SHIN-TAKATSUKA HUT	YAKENO JUNCTION

A1 O1 —— ● —— ● —— ● —— M1 —— Y1 N1

35 min ⇨ 105 min ⇨ 10 min ⇨ 70 min ⇨ 250 min

25 min ⇦ 85 min ⇦ 10 min ⇦ 60 min ⇦ 150 min

OKABU TRAIL (O1)

The trail entrance is little more than a modern toilet building across a short bridge and a sign pointing to raised wooden steps up into the forest. There is a sign in Japanese here and to save you scratching your head wondering whether it says anything important. Here is a short translation of what it informs tired hikers:

- The path becomes steep from here on.
- You should leave this point before 10.00 as it takes 4 hours to make the return trip from here from Jomon Sugi.
- You should leave Jomon Sugi at 13.00 to return to this point in good time especially if you have a health condition or in bad weather.
- You should visit the toilet here as it is the only regular toilet before

Jomon Sugi.

• You should not leave any rubbish.

It is a short 30 minute (400 m) slog up from this sign to the remains of **Okina sugi** (翁杉). This was until 2010 a great Yakusugi that stood at 24 m and was thought to be 2,000 years old. The mostly hollow base however could not hold the tree's weight and all but 3 m of it collapsed.

Depending on the time you come, you may be passing many exhausted hikers already digging into their food supplies but you are only 200 m from another major milestone on the route:

Wilson's Stump (ウィルソン株). Although sounding like a rather nasty medical complaint, it is in fact a tree stump so large (a circumference of 13.8m) that it contains within it a shrine and a stream.

The tree that stood here is thought to have been cut down on the orders of Hideyoshi Toyotomi (1536-1598) in 1586, and it was not until a British botanist named Ernest Henry Wilson (1876-1930) was led to the stump that it was introduced to the rest of the world in 1914 and like many other species he introduced from Asia, bears his name. Because of the numbers of people passing through this way you can no longer get close. There is a sign in Japanese which tells people not to camp in this area, not to go too near to the stump, not to start any fires and generally to be considerate to other hikers. It is a popular place to stop so if you want to experience it quietly see it early morning or late afternoon.

The trail then becomes a mixture of wooden platforms and forest floor as you pass some of the other grand Yakusugi trees at an altitude of 1200-1300 m. **Daio-sugi** (大王杉) is 1 hour 10 min (1 km) further down the track. It is estimated to be 3,000 years old and it is largely hollow at its 11.1 m diameter base. Shortly after (100 m) you are greeted by a pair of trees called **Meoto-sugi** (夫婦杉). The 'husband' tree is on the right and is thicker in diameter than the 'wife' on the left who in turn is taller. The husband is thought to be 2,000 years old with a 10.9 m circumference and the wife slightly younger at 1,500 years old but standing at 25.5 m high. A horizontal branch has grown between them to join the two trunks together hence the coupling of the trees.

There are several piped drinking water springs – watch out for them on the way and keep filling up your water supplies. Again, it will seem like forever but, after only another 30 min (700 m), one of the bends in the path will bring you to a large raised platform in front of which is the holy grail of Yakusugi trees, **Jomon Sugi** (縄文杉).

It depends on whole range of factors as to how impressed you will be by visiting the most famous tree of all. The weather, the time, the amount of people (up to 500 people a day visit the tree), your level of exhaustion and the distance you are from the tree (15 m) – these all make a difference. Like Wilson's Stump, if you want the tree all to yourself, late afternoon and early morning are better.

Hikers are restricted to the platform due to the damage done by the ever increasing numbers of tourists. Remember the tree is a national treasure so do not attempt to get any closer to it. Souvenir-hunting tourists scraped a piece of bark (10 x 10 cm) from the tree in 2005 which made national news and re-quired experts from all over Japan to ensure the tree's survival.

A covered shelter is

just around the bend after Jomon sugi and then it is a short 10 min hike (200 m) to the **Takatsuka Hut** (高塚小屋) and fresh drinking water. This hut was rebuilt in 2013 with sustainable materials and sleeps up to 20 hikers. For obvious reasons this hut is popular and can fill up quickly in high season so a second larger hut (which fits 40) was built in 1992, an hour (1 km) up the path, and is called the **Shin-Takatsuka Hut** (新高塚小屋). If you ing water. This hut was rebuilt in 2013 with sustainable materials and sleeps up to 20 hikers. For obvious reasons this hut is popular and can fill up quickly in high season so a second larger hut (which fits 40) was built in 1992, an hour (1 km) up the path, and is called the **Shin-Takatsuka Hut** (新高塚小屋). If you are continuing up to Miyanoura dake along the Miyanoura Trail (M1) this may be a better choice.

It is important not under-estimate the A1 and O1 trails up to Jomon Sugi. It is not a gentle wander through the forest but places you high in the central mountains (Jomon Sugi is at 1280 m) and walking a distance of 10.6 km one way in sometimes difficult terrain. It is necessary to be prepared with proper equipment and supplies (see the hiking equipment section) and the trail can also sometimes be slippery and potentially dangerous with many of the bridges holding little or no protection from falling.

Despite the potential dangers, hikers of all ages manage to success-fully complete this trail, including children, and with good preparation it is a reasonable day trip. Overall, the trail can be incredibly monotonous in places, especially the railroad, but as there are no sweeping views on the trail, it is still perfectly fine to hike if it is raining,

In fact, try not be too disheartened if the weather closes in, the forest can often be just as beautiful in the rain. And unless you are particularly interested in the local flora and fauna or have health and safety concerns, a guide is not necessary as the trail is clearly marked all the way. Try to see it very early or very late in the day before or after the tour groups spoil the peace with their chatter and bright raincoats.

MIYANOURA TRAIL (M1)

If you are descending along the Miyanoura Trail from Miyanoura dake you will find it considerably less arduous and much quicker (you save 1 hour) than ascending from Shin-Takatsuka Hut (新高塚小屋). Coming up is a hard slog as you leave the tree line and head closer to the high mountains but it is a very common route for hikers who first went to Jomon sugi and now would like to visit Miyanoura dake.

If you are descending from Miyanoura dake, it is a steep climb down

A gift for you

Aunt Mary and Uncle Dick, This little guide book is a mix of pictures and facts about a magical little Japanese island. Love, Michael initially and then a more gentle gradient before becoming steep again. There is a water source 500 m down the trail.

If you are ascending from Shin-Takatsuka Hut, make sure you fill up your water containers as there is no fresh water sources for at least 3 hours as you steadily climb upwards.

There are two waypoints on the trail. The lower waypoint is **Dai-ichi Tenboudai** (第一展望台) (80 min from Shin-Takatsuka Hut/100 min from Yakeno junction) and the higher waypoint is **Hiraishi Tenboudai** (平石 展望台), a lookout point with wonderful views and a stream for water (210 min from Shin-Takatsuka Hut/30 min from Yakeno junction).

1 km from the summit of Miyanoura dake is the junction with the Nagata Trail (N1), called **Yakeno Sansaro or Junction** (焼野三叉路). If you wish to climb up to Nagata dake from this intersection, it is not as easy as the 1.5 km distance might appear. The trail is often overgrown and you need to descend and then re-ascend all over again in the short distance between the two peaks. If you have the energy, it is worthwhile. In all it should take around 50 min from the junction to the summit of **Nagata dake.** On a clear day you can look down on Nagata village and far into the East China Sea and to your right is **Shojidake** (障子岳), a distinctive wall-like mountain that drops into the valley. Especially in summer be careful of over exposure to the sun as there is little shade at this altitude. Also if you are returning to the Yodogawa entrance be prepared with a flashlight just in case it takes longer than you had planned. If you are staying in the **Shikanosawa Hut,**

there is still a way to go from the summit of Nagata dake, so give yourself enough time to cover the 1.2 km (around 70 min). It is easy to reach the summit and believe that you have arrived at your destination only to be in despair when you have to walk for another hour. If you plan to continue onwards from here see Nagata Trail (N1) details.

Y1 YODOGAWA TRAIL 淀川歩道

DIFFICULTY: 🐵 🐵 🐵

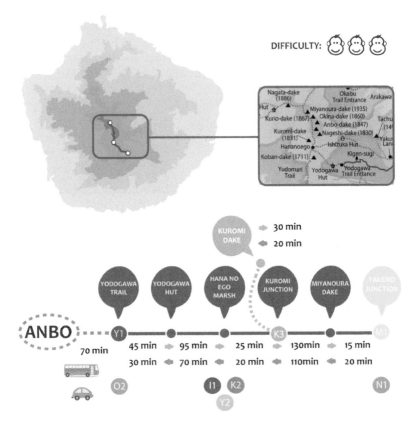

CAR: The road after Yakusugiland winds up, twisting and turning its way to Kigen sugi (紀元杉) which stands beside the road, accessible by wooden steps. From then on the road is narrow until the small car park and toilet block at the end which is often full by day-break. If so, park at the nearest safe place on the main road. It should take 30 min by car from Yakusugiland.

BUS: Take the bus to No.72 Kigen sugi (紀元杉) bus stop and continue on the road or alternatively go on foot from Yakusugiland for 8 km (2½ hours).

Yodogawa Trail Entrance (淀川登山口) begins with wooden steps up into the forest. It then alternates with wooden steps or platforms and the forest floor for much of the 1.5 km (45 min) to **Yodogawa Hut** (淀川小屋). There is fresh water in the stream behind – go through the gap in the trees to the left of the hut. There is also a toilet across the path from the hut and flat land to cook or eat on. It is usually very popular and can get busy at the end of the day.

Once you cross the river the path is relentlessly uphill, zigzagging its way upwards. Occasionally it becomes very steep and there are ropes to help you clamber up the rocks, but nothing overly risky, even for children.

After around 90 min the path will level out and through the gaps in the trees on your left you will begin to glimpse a strange curiosity at the top of one of the lower peaks. This is **Koban dake** (高盤岳) and famously looks like chopped tofu. It marks the fact that you are now at **Hana-no-ego Marsh** (花之江河), the southern-most highland natural marsh in Japan.

 Hana-no-ego Marsh is a wetland of international importance and home to Tago's brown frog (ヤクシマタゴガエル), a native subspecies and they can be seen lurking just below the water. It is also the only known home to a freshwater shellfish, 'Pisidium habei' (ハベマメシジミ). It is a common sight to see deer grazing around the marsh as you walk on the raised planks and you can stop at the occasional viewing platform.

There are three other trails that lead off from the marsh. To the left is the **Yudomari Trail** (Y2) (湯泊歩道) / **Kurio Trail** (K2) (栗生歩道) which both lead all the way down to the coast. To the right is the 50 min trail to the **Ishizuka Hut** (I1) (石塚小屋) and on from that a further 7 km to Yakusugiland. The central mountains are all located on the main trail which bends to the left and to the right but is essentially straight on.

It is now just a short way (25 min) to the intersection for **Kuromi dake** (黒味岳) at 1831 m. It comes after a large rock and is signposted to the left. This detour takes you on the **Kuromi Trail** (K3) via ropes and some scrambling (30 min) to the top of Kuromi dake and gives you sweeping 360° views. It is a good spot for photos of Miyanoura dake and for surveying the path that leads ahead above the tree line. For those who have had enough of trekking at this point, this is a popular destination in itself.

Soon after the turn off to Kuromi the path brings you above the tree line. If the weather is clear, there should be beautiful views as you follow the trail upwards.

Keep slogging on (there are still 3 km to go) and you end up ascending as much as you are descending as the path cuts a fairly straight line at various proximities to the ridge line of the summits of **Nageishi dake** (投石岳) at 1830 m, **Anbo dake** (安房岳) at 1847 m, **Okina dake** (翁岳) at 1860 m, and **Kurio dake** (栗生岳) at 1867 m. At this height, the trees have given

way to grassland and most of it is small evergreen bamboo grass, native to Yakushima, and known as 'dwarf bamboo'. There are also Yakushima Rhododendrons which bloom in late spring/early summer and an officially organised hike called 'Shakunage Tozan' marks the beginning of their blooming season.

As you continue on the trail, the landscape gradually becomes more barren and the presence of many windswept Yakusugi skeleton trees give it an altogether different feel to the forest below you.

The final climb up to the peak of **Miyanoura dake** (宮之浦岳) at 1935 m is a steep one. There are a number of small caves and a shrine

on the way in which you can shelter should the weather take a turn for the worse. When you do finally reach the top there are enough rocks to break the wind but no covered shelter. On a clear day the views of the whole island and beyond are spectacular.

Some hikers then continue on either to **Nagata dake** (永田岳) which stands at 1886 m with the option of staying at the **Shikanosawa Hut** (鹿之沢小屋) along the N1 Trail or descend along the M1 Trail to the **Shin-Takatsuka Hut** (新高塚小屋) towards Jomon Sugi.

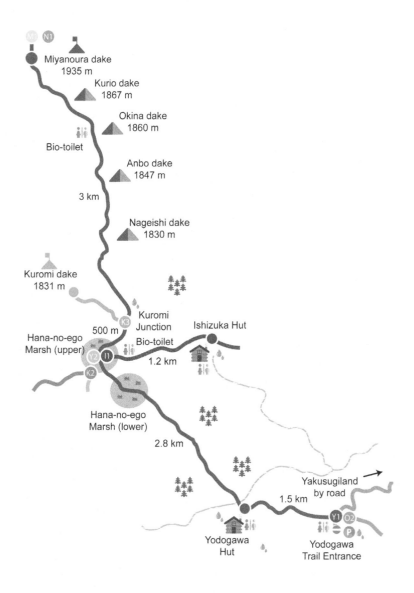

M1 N1
● Miyanoura dake
1935 m

▲ Kurio dake
1867 m

▲ Okina dake
1860 m

🚻 Bio-toilet

▲ Anbo dake
1847 m

3 km

▲ Nageishi dake
1830 m

Kuromi dake
1831 m

K3 Kuromi
Junction
500 m

Hana-no-ego
Marsh (upper)   Bio-toilet   Ishizuka Hut

Y2 I1   🚻   1.2 km

K2

Hana-no-ego
Marsh (lower)

2.8 km

Yakusugiland
by road

1.5 km

Y1 O2
P

Yodogawa
Hut

Yodogawa
Trail Entrance

K1 KUSUGAWA TRAIL 楠川歩道

DIFFICULTY:

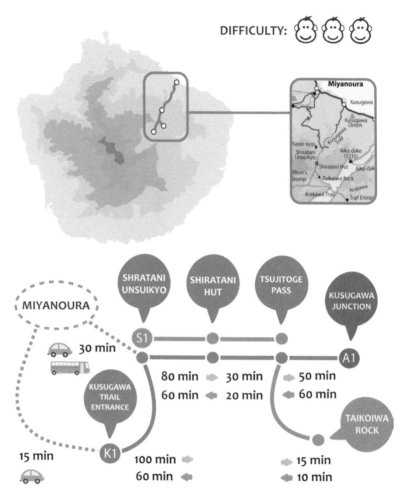

CAR: The road is signed towards the mountain from the main road in Kusugawa. Follow the single lane road to the end where there is a sign for the Kusugawa Mountain Trail Entrance (楠川登山道入口). There is no real car park as such but park your car at the side where the road ends.
BUS: Get off at No.37 Kusugawa (楠川) bus stop, a few kilometres south from Miyanoura. The trail is clearly signed on the mountain side of the main road and it is a 1 hour walk from the bus stop to the trail entrance (3.2 km).

The K1 Trail begins near the coast and is a useful hiking alternative to taking the mountain road up or down to/from Shiratani Unsuikyo (S1). The trail is initially paved from the trail entrance but soon you reach the canopy of the forest and underfoot is nothing but the dirt of the forest floor. Occasionally logging takes place in this area so there may be machinery or signs of tree cutting dotted around.

It is a relatively simple trail to follow as it was part of the main Edo Period (1603 - 1868) logging path and along the way you will come across the brick remains of charcoal ovens and other leftovers from a bygone age when logging was still the main industry on Yakushima.

There are rarely more than a handful of hikers who take this trail and there are often macaques and deer foraging nearby. Pink ribbons mark the trail upwards and it is quite steep and sometimes slightly overgrown but eventually (after 1½ hours) you should reach a gravel road. It would be much easier on your legs and faster to take the trail down rather than up.

At the road, you have a choice of going right to the entrance of Shiratani Unsuikyo (with toilets and buses) or

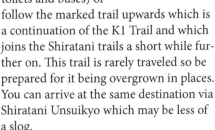

follow the marked trail upwards which is a continuation of the K1 Trail and which joins the Shiratani trails a short while further on. This trail is rarely traveled so be prepared for it being overgrown in places. You can arrive at the same destination via Shiratani Unsuikyo which may be less of a slog.

The rest of the K1 Trail is well trodden and will take you upwards on a clear stone trail through Shiratani Unsuikyo

Shiratani
Unsuikyo

2.1 km

Shiratani
Hut

1.1 km

Tsujitoge
Pass

Taikoiwa
Rock

1.4 km

(S1), past **Shiratani Hut** over **Tsuji-toge pass** (and the side trip to Tai-koiwa Rock - see S1 for more details) and descends rapidly to join the forest railroad and the A1 Trail after 50 min (1.4 km).

On the way down to the A1 trail you will pass **Tsuji Grotto** (辻の岩屋) which is the gap created between a horizontal laying giant boulder and the rocks it rests on. It can fit 5-6 people underneath and is used as an emergency mountain shelter.

This route from Shiratani over Tsujitoge pass is often used as an alternative to the Arakawa Trail (A1) and the Okabu Trail (O1) to Jomon Sugi and Mi-yanoura dake. It is particularly useful when the higher mountain

roads are impassable. It also means that the route to/from Jomon Sugi is walkabkle directly to/from the coast.

S1 SHIRATANI UNSUIKYO 白谷雲水峡

DIFFICULTY:

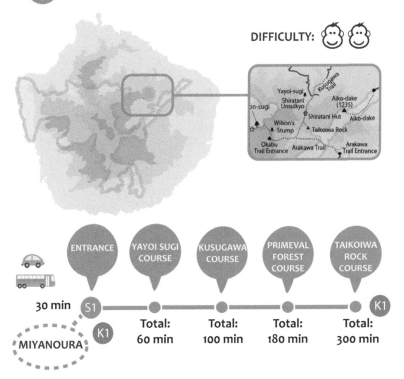

CAR: The mountain road is clearly sign posted (in English) from Route 77 in Miyanoura. Route 594 meanders up for 12 km, climbs 800 m and takes around 30 min by car. The road has been improved over the past few years but there are still some tight spots higher up where it is still single track. The free car park is past the entrance hut and over the bridge, although if it is full you have to park on the main road leading up to the park.

BUS: There are several buses a day from Miyanoura and the journey takes 30 minutes. Get off at the last stop - No.29 Shiratani Unsuikyo bus stop.

Shiratani Unsuikyo centres on a tributary of Miyanoura river and covers over 420 hectares of evergreen broad leaf forest. The entrance is at 620 m and consists of a collection of wooden huts which mark the beginning of the trail. If you enter here you have to pay ¥300 (but not if you keep to the K1 Trail). The toilets are across the bridge on the way from the main car park.

A large map stands at the entrance of Shiratani Unsuikyo. It details the routes of several colour-coded courses to follow. If you come via the main entrance and pay the entrance fee, you are given a map (in English) of all the routes. The **Yayoisugi Cedar Trail** is 60 min and can be done in normal footwear, but the **Kusugawa Trail** (1 hour 40 min), the **Primeval Forest Trail** (3 hour) and the **Taikoiwa Rock Trail** (5 hours) all ideally require proper mountain shoes and basic equipment like waterproofs, a backpack, food and a container for water (see the hiking equipment section for more details). Having said that, it is not that uncommon to see people hiking in flip-flops and all manner of inappropriate attire.

The trail follows the river for the first section of steps and walkways. After a short while there will be a fork to the right to **Yayoi sugi** (弥生杉). This is worth the 500 m detour as it is one of the oldest Yakusugi at 3,000 years of age. The path consists of platforms and stone steps and although you can no longer touch it, you can get close enough. Late afternoon or early morning you should have the tree all to yourself.

If you take the side trail to Yayoi sugi you can continue on the same trail and after 600 m you will re-join the main trail further up. If you do this, you avoid a giant rock called **Oiwa Rest Place** (憩いの大岩) on the main trail where the wooden steps give way to climbing up the rock face for a few meters.

The wooden steps begin again soon after and when both trails have met again, the main feature in this part of Shiratani is the waterfall which runs to the side of the trail called **Hiryu Otoshi** (飛流おとし). In rainy

season the water gushes down, but at other times you can get closer and follow stone steps on to the rocks. If you keep climbing, you come to the end of the tree covered path where the Satsuki-tsuribashi (さつき吊橋) suspension bridge crosses the valley.

From here there are 2 options:

1. Cross the bridge and you will come to an extension of the **Kusugawa Trail** (楠川歩道) that began down at the coast (See K1 Trail for more details) and which continues up to **Shiratani Hut** (

白谷小屋) and beyond. The trail was laid in the Edo period and is fairly straight and solid. You have to cross one river on stepping stones so proceed with caution after rain.

2. Do not cross the bridge and continue straight ahead for a meandering hike through pristine damp forest with uneven trails and rivers to hop over. This is the **Genseirin (Primeval Forest) Trail** (原生林歩道).

In the end both trails meet in the same place, at the foot of the short trail to Shiratani Hut.

PRIMEVAL FOREST TRAIL

Be cautious after rain on this trail as the river levels can make it hazardous but the forest in this area is what you might see in magazines and postcards about Yakushima and it also includes several important yakusugi trees. If you wanted to go no further up the mountain, this trail can be a worthwhile circular trip, returning to Shiratani Unsuikyo entrance on the Kusugawa trail.

Around 200 m along the trail is the second of the grand cedars, **Nidai-Osugi** (二代大杉). It stands above a small stream and at 32 m, is one of the tallest Yakusugi in Shiratani. '二代' means 'second generation' and the tree is the product of germination on top of a fallen cedar. Over the years the original tree decayed and the gap is left where that tree once stood.

The trail then snakes its way up for the next 500 m to **Sanbonashi-sugi** (三本足杉) which stands like a tripod on the forest floor. Its strange shape is due to the same process as that of Nidai-Osugi. The host tree fell, the second generation cedar grew over it and when the host tree decayed and withered away, the open space remained.

You soon have to cross a bridgeless river and care must be taken especially after heavy rain. You

Taikoiwa Rock

A1

Tsujitoge Pass

Nanahonsugi

Shiratani Hut

Kugurisugi

Nidai-kugurisugi

Primeval Forest Trail

Sanbon-yarisugi

Caution after heavy rain

Kusugawa Trail

Bugyosugi

Bibinkosugi

Sanbonashi-sugi

Satsuki-tsurihashi Bridge

Nidai-osugi

Yayoi Trail

Yayoisugi

Entrance

S1

Kusugawa Trail

Miyanoura by road

K1

P

P

have to jump from rock to rock but keep an eye out for the pink ribbons to keep on the trail.

The next tree, **Bibinkosugi** (びびんこ杉), is 100 m further on. This is a young sugi at just 350 years old and its name was chosen in 1999 by a local junior high school teacher, Takeshi Wakita (脇田武志). 'びびんこ' means 'piggy-back' (肩車) in Kagoshima dialect and was chosen to reflect the second generation growth so common in the sugi trees in Yakushima.

The trail then makes a gradual turn towards **San-bonyari-sugi** (三本槍杉) which means '3 spears sugi' and its name becomes clear when you see that three trees appear to stem from one slanted trunk. The host tree is thought to be around 800 years old but two of the 'spears' are second generation cedars, the third is actually thought to be one of the original branches.

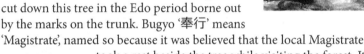

Continue on and **Bugyosugi** (奉行杉) lies across another river. There was an attempt to cut down this tree in the Edo period borne out by the marks on the trunk. Bugyo '奉行' means 'Magistrate', named so because it was believed that the local Magistrate took a rest beside the tree while visiting the forest. It is not particularly tall at 24 m but it makes up for this in trunk thickness with a circumference of 8.5 m.

Nidai-Kugurisugi (二代くぐり杉) is soon before the branch of the trail that leads up towards Shiratani Hut and you will find yourself walking through its trunk.

You have the choice here of continuing on the same trail which will bring you back to Shiratani Unsuikyo Entrance or take the trail upwards through the two giant legs of **Kugurisugi** (くぐり杉) before the ground levels off and **Shiratani Hut** (白谷小屋) is signed to your right.

SHIRATANI HUT

At Shiratani Hut there is a river for drinking water, shelter if you need it and a not too pleasant smelling toilet within. There is a large communal area inside and there are a few separate rooms to sleep in. Outside there are some large tables and benches to sit on. It is a popular place for deer and they can often be spotted munching away amongst the trees.

TAIKOIWA ROCK

The main destination after Shiratani Hut is **Taikoiwa Rock** (太鼓岩), a 45 minute hike further up the mountain. The trail becomes steeper and rocky as it rises but the forest opens out and there is more a feeling of space.

Soon you will pass **Nanahonsugi** (七本杉), a cedar so named because of its seven branches, although two have dropped off over the years now leaving only five. You will then come across what was temporarily known as Mononoke forest. So named because of the local connection with the Ghibli studios' animated movie 'Princess Mononoke' (もののけ姫). It has since been renamed due to copyright but anyway, this is more a creation for tired, hurried tourists who need a goal to walk to rather than a particularly beautiful piece of forest. If you took the 150 minute course to get there you would have seen far more beautiful sights.

When you reach the top of the trail, the 979 m high point of **Tsujitoge Pass** (辻峠), there are some wooden benches and signs in Japanese. Taikoiwa Rock is to the left with two short paths and the Tsujitoge pass continues straight on. To climb up to Taikoiwa

Rock you are supposed to ascend on the path furthest from you (to the right) and return on the one nearest (to the left). You may get some grumbling from stumbling hikers and their guides if you choose the wrong one. The trees are tightly packed and the going is very hard but it is only a short distance (15 min) before you reach the gap in the undergrowth and you are breathtakingly surveying the whole of the central mountain range with Anbo River gushing in the distance.

Hana-no-ego
& Ishizuka Hut

Tachu dake
1497 m

Mitsunesugi

Hahakosugi

Tenmon
Forest

Sawatsubashi
Bridge

Tenchusugi

Tenchubashi
Bridge

T1

Jamonsugi

Tsutsujigawara

Bio-toilet

Kokenohashi
Bridge

Higechoro-sugi

Kohana trail

Tachu Junction

Buddhasugi

Arakawabashi
bridge

Sennensugi

Futagosugi

Kuguritsuga

Entrance

Anbo

Y3

Kugurisugi

Shinsen
Resthouse

Risenkyo
Bridge

P

Exit

Seiryobashi Bridge

P

Kigensugi

- As the 50 min course until **Arakawa Hiking Trail** (荒川歩道)
- **Arakawa Bridge** (荒川橋)
- **Tachu Junction** (太忠分れ) is the turn off from the trail to the right for the 150 min course and **Tachu dake** (T1). Soon after the path comes close to the river and this is a

perfect spot for a break on the large rocks spanning across the water.
• **Kokenohashi Bridge** (苔の橋) means 'moss' bridge and has a shelter with a bench on the opposite side
• **Tsutsujigawara** (つつじ河原) is a lookout point with a small round shelter
• **Sawatsubashi Bridge** (沢津橋) crosses Arakawa River again
• **Buddhasugi** (仏陀杉) then follow the 50 min course.

150 MIN COURSE

This course leads you much deeper through the forest.
• As the 80 min course until **Tachu Junction** (太忠分れ)
• **Kohana Hiking Trail** (小花歩道) which passes through the 'giant tree' forest of **Kobannayama** (小花山).
• **Higechoro-sugi** (ひげ長老) was named by a local Elementary school student (who won the official naming competition) because the moss at the bottom of the tree resembled an old man's beard.
• Portable Bio-toilet
• **Jamonsugi** (蛇紋杉) is near the rest hut at the trail junction. This giant cedar tree was blown down in Sept 1997 by Typhoon No.19 and the tangle of roots weave outwards like a sculpture
• **Tenchubashi Bridge** (天柱橋) used to be made from cedar wood but was washed away in a typhoon
• **Tenchusugi** (天柱杉) is 1,500 years old and at 33.8 m is one of the tallest yakusugi in Yakushima
• **Hahakosugi** (母子杉) - '母' means mother and '子' child and these two cedar trees are so named because they have grown so close to each other. Both are around 2,600 years old. The mother is 31.1 m tall (but has already died) and the child slightly shorter at 29 m
• **Mitsunesugi** (三根杉) is the thickest of all the Yakusugi in Yakusugiland with a diameter of 9.3 m but it is one of the youngest at a sprightly 1,100 years old.
• **Sawatsubashi Bridge** (沢津橋) then follow the 80 min course.

There are also 2 mountain trails which begin at Yakusugiland: T1 trail and I1 Trail. The former is a well-hiked trail to a high viewpoint and the latter, a tough trail leading into the high mountains.

T1 TACHU DAKE TRAIL 太忠岳歩道

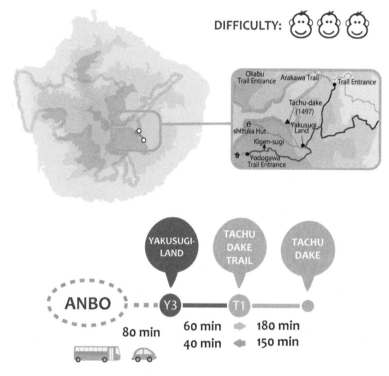

DIFFICULTY: 🐵 🐵 🐵

Take the 150 minute hiking course in Yakusugiland and when you cross the Arakawa Bridge take the Kohana Trail for around 500 m to the shelter. Here the path turns sharply left and the trail to Tachu dake is signed straight on and upwards.

The mistake that many people make is to underestimate the Tachu dake Trail. It rises up to 1497 m and consists of very steep and rough terrain including ropes and ladders. It is easy to just continue on believing it to be an extension of the Yakusugiland path but be warned, you need lots of time and energy for it to be an enjoyable experience and not a hard slog.

The trail is clearly marked all the way but is very steep in places and sometimes requires scrambling on all fours. Water is

Tenchuseki

Ishizuka
Junction

Tachu-dake
1497 m

2.5 km

Tenmon
Forest

T1

Kohana
Trail

Yakusugiland   Y3

available in two streams that run after the
rest area of **Tenmon Forest** (天文の森)
where there is a sign and benches. It then
climbs up to a giant boulder which the
path skirts around and continues up.

The trail then rises very steeply on the
way to **Ishizuka Junction** (石塚分かれ)
where the path veers left but then makes
a sharp right turn. There is an overgrown
trail from this point to the nearby mountain of **Hanaoredake** (花折岳) but with
no public access.

The trail is then a
matter of climbing up
ladders and ropes un-
til you see the rocks
at the summit. It can
be confusing when
you reach the summit

as the path drops down to the side of the
bare rock. There is however a rope with
which you can pull yourself up to the
huge horizontal stone that points out east-
wards to Anbo and the sea in the distance.
The large rock behind it that points up to
the sky is known as **Tenchuseki**.

The view from here is well worth the
climb and is nothing short of spectacular
on a clear day.

I1 ISHIZUKA TRAIL 石塚歩道

DIFFICULTY: 😊 😊 😊 😊

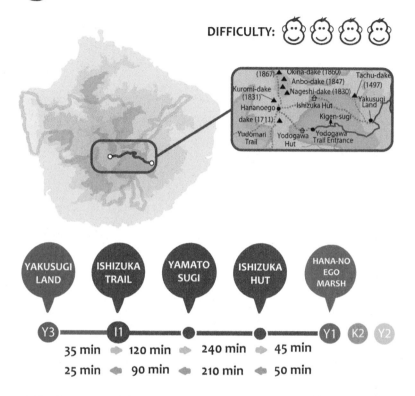

YAKUSUGI LAND	ISHIZUKA TRAIL	YAMATO SUGI	ISHIZUKA HUT	HANA-NO EGO MARSH

Y3 — I1 — ● — ● — Y1 K2 Y2

35 min ➡ 120 min ➡ 240 min ➡ 45 min
25 min ⬅ 90 min ⬅ 210 min ⬅ 50 min

Take the 150 min hiking course in Yakusugiland and 300 m after Tenchu Bridge (天柱橋) there is a sign to **Hana-no-ego Marsh** (花之江河) to the right (see Y3 map).

From here to the **Ishizuka Hut** is a 6 hour slog up an underused path and through several un-bridged rivers.

On the way (after around 2 hours) you will come across **Yamato sugi** (大和杉) on your left, a grand Yakusugi tree which stands at around 35 m and is estimated to be 3-4,000 years old. From the hut it is a further 45 min before you reach Hana-no-ego Marsh.

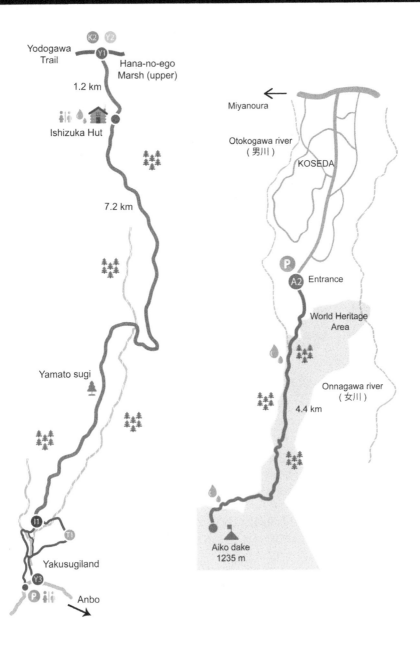

Yodogawa Trail

K2 Y2

Y1

Hana-no-ego Marsh (upper)

1.2 km

Ishizuka Hut

7.2 km

Yamato sugi

I1

T1

Yakusugiland

Y3

P

Anbo

Miyanoura

Otokogawa river (男川)

KOSEDA

P

A2 Entrance

World Heritage Area

Onnagawa river (女川)

4.4 km

Aiko dake 1235 m

AIKO DAKE TRAIL 愛子岳歩道

DIFFICULTY: ☺ ☺ ☺

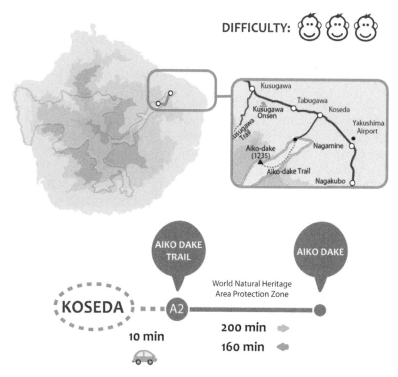

CAR: Signed on Route 77 at the south end of Koseda village. Turn inland and follow the narrow road through gradually thicker forest until you come across the Aiko dake Trail Entrance sign (愛子岳登山口). It is about a 10 min drive. There is a small parking area to the right just before.

BUS: Get off at No.43 Nishi Koseda (西小瀬田) bus stop on the main coastal road and walk past the convenience store. Turn inland at the sign and walk 2.6 km to the trail entrance.

The attraction of scaling Aiko dake is that almost the whole path is within the **World Natural Heritage Area Protection Zone**. It is also, however, one of the toughest day hikes on the island. You might notice that I have only given it 3 monkeys, rather than 4, for difficulty as you do not need any particular hiking or climbing skills to follow the trail, you just need to be relatively fit and be prepared to be exhausted by the time you return.

From the outset, you ascend through thick forest and relentlessly climb for two hours until just over 1,000 m. Every few hundred meters there are height markers to inform you of the altitude and once at the highest point a short descent then lulls you into thinking you are almost there but then you have to clamber on your hands and knees over the last even steeper rocky ascent.

There is a small drinkable stream about ½ an hour after the trail veers right (it does this at 984 m).

The summit (1235 m) has a series of ropes to pull yourself up a fairly steep rock face and once there you are rewarded with magnificent views of the coast and of the higher inland mountains.

Due to the exposed nature of the summit, it is probably best to avoid it on gusty days.

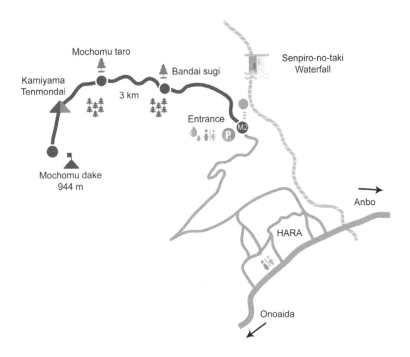

M2 MOCHOMU TRAIL モッチョム岳歩道

DIFFICULTY: 😊 😊 😊

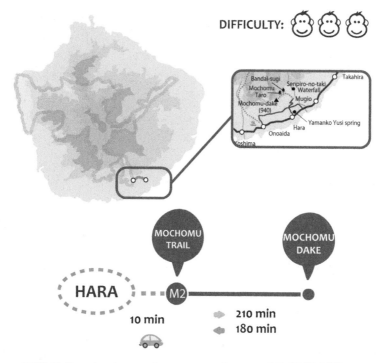

CAR: Follow the signs to Senpiro-no-taki Waterfall (千尋の滝) at Hara (原). There are several routes from the main road all leading to the same windy 3 km road. Midway it makes a tight right turn but continue until you reach the car park and souvenir store. The trail entrance is on the path to the waterfall viewing area.

BUS: Get off at any one of 3 bus stops in or near Hara. Either get off at No.87 Tainokawa (鯛ノ川) bus stop and walk 300m across the bridge to the signed right turn; Or get off at No.88 Hara Iriguchi (原入口) and walk (Onoaida direction) until the park where you turn right; Or get off at No.89 Hara (原) and walk (Anbo direction) to the park where you turn left. Whichever stop you get off at it is 3 km (50 min) to the water-fall (and trail entrance).

Another very tough hike is to scale the lump of rock that hangs over Onoaida called Mochomu Dake (944 m). The trail begins at the short paved road from the car park to the viewing place at Senpiro-no-taki

Waterfall.

Midway along there is a sign to the left and a trail into the trees. The climb is very steep initially but levels off and then is intermittently steep, often requiring scrambling up on all fours.

After 1½ hours you reach the first of two notable trees, **Bandai Sugi** (万代杉), estimated to be 3,000 years old. While its trunk is a solid 8.6 m thickness, it stands at a modest height of only 13 m probably due to exposure to the strong coastal winds. If you look closely it shows evidence of Edo period logging. This is followed by the much taller **Mochomu Taro** (モッチョム太郎) which reaches 24 m in height, it too has the scars of loggers.

Once you reach **Kamiyama Tembodai** (神山展望台), a viewpoint at the highest point of the trail, an hour later, you then actually start descending for the last 500 m to the summit of Mochomu dake.

The path is usually very quiet and it can be slightly overgrown outside of summer but is easy to follow and there are spectacular views from the top on a clear day.

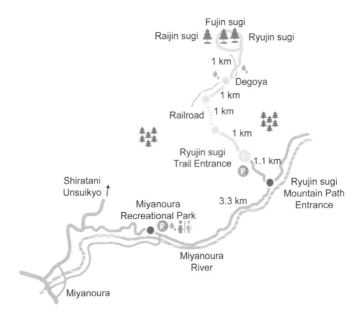

R1 RYUJINSUGI TRAIL 龍神杉登山道

DIFFICULTY: ☺ ☺ ☺

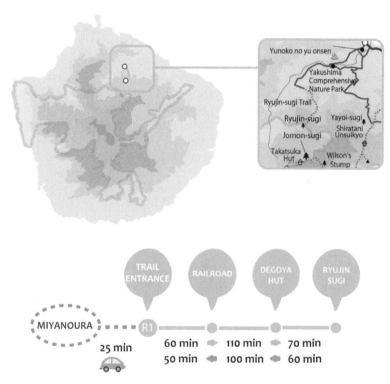

Yunoko no yu onsen
Yakushima Comprehensive Nature Park
Ryujin-sugi Trail
Ryujin-sugi   Yayoi-sugi
Jomon-sugi   Shiratani Unsuikyo
Takatsuka Hut   Wilson's Stump

TRAIL ENTRANCE · RAILROAD · DEGOYA HUT · RYUJIN SUGI

MIYANOURA · · · R1

25 min 🚗

60 min ➡ 110 min ➡ 70 min
50 min ⬅ 100 min ⬅ 60 min

CAR: From Yakushima Comprehensive Nature Park (屋久島総合自然公) take the small road next to and on the same side of the river (神之川林道). After 3 km there is a left turn with a sign for Ryujin sugi Trail Entrance (龍神杉登山口) and a very steep hill. This hill will lead you the 1 km to the trail head (歩道入口). The road is unpaved and will be bumpy without a 4WD. It is possible to park near the trail (limited spaces) although sometimes there are obstructions in the road or you can park back in the car park of Yakushima Comprehensive Nature Park and walk one hour to the trail head.

BUS: Get off at No.31 Miyanoura Sho (宮之浦小) bus stop and take the mountain road towards Shiratani Unsuikyo. After crossing a river the road steeply rises and bends to the right. Turn right at the sign for Yakushima Comprehensive Nature Park and when you reach the car park at the end (30 min), continue on the unpaved forest road that runs parallel to the river as above.

This trail is the old Yakusando Trail (益救参道登) which has been renamed 'Ryujin sugi' (龍神杉), after the Yakusugi tree at the end of the trail. It is an older path with is not traversed very often and it is more than likely that you will be the only one on it.

For the first hour the trail gently climbs through open forest until at an altitude of around 600 m, the remains of the old logging station (造林小屋跡) leads you on to the disused forest railroad (トロッコ軌道跡). This is from a time when 4 separate forest railroads transported Yakushima's trees down to the coast but now has a ghostly feel to it with discarded items littering the forest floor.

Follow the railroad track for 20 min and where trees block you from going any further there is a very steep trail to the right. From here onwards, it is relentlessly upwards but the path is clear and not too taxing. After 1½ hours you cross a river and then a very spooky mountain lodge, **Degoya Hut** (出小屋跡), which has collapsed spilling out the belongings of long departed mountain workers. You then cross the same river again but caution is advised here after heavy rain as it can be dangerous. It then becomes steeper again as you climb the last 1 km to the three **Sanjin Sugi** (三神杉) trees known individually as **Dragon Ryujin Sugi** (龍神杉), **Thunder & Lightning Raijin Sugi** (雷神杉) and **Wind Fujin Sugi** (風神杉). There are wooden platforms and steps guiding you on a circular

tour of the trees. Go left and as the trail rises, Raijin sugi and Fujin sugi are either side of the trail opposite each other.

The left tree is Raijin sugi as it has the marks of a lightning strike at the rear. When the trail veers right you have reached the end and there is a platform facing the magnificent Ryujin sugi. There is a branch of the trail from here which used to lead to Jomon Sugi however the trail is overgrown and no longer used.

O2 ONOAIDA TRAIL   尾之間歩道

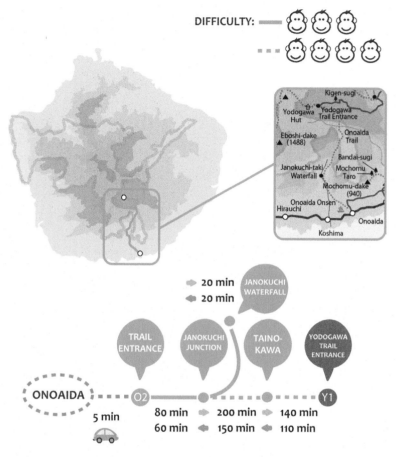

DIFFICULTY:

CAR: Follow signs for Onoaida Onsen (尾之間温泉). At the traffic signals at the far end of Onoaida bypass turn inland and the onsen is at the end of the narrow road. You can park in the car park to the left of the Onsen.

BUS: Get off at No.98 Onoaida Onsen Iriguchi (尾之間温泉入口) bus stop and it is a 20 min walk inland from the traffic signals to the Onsen and the trail head.

There are two parts to this trail depending on how far you wish to walk. Most hikers take the trail as far as Janokuchi Waterfall and then return but the main trail continues high up into the central mountain range and can be the start of a much longer trip. If you have a copy of the Lonely Planet Hiking Guide, you may have spotted this route as part of a trans-Yakushima hike. The Tourist Information Office stress that this is NOT a good idea. The Onoaida Trail after Janokuchi Waterfall is very tough and potentially dangerous and there have been several accidents. There are so many trails to choose from on Yakushima, so either think about a safer combination or make sure you are thoroughly prepared, with the right mountain equipment and with up-to-date trail reports and weather forecasts.

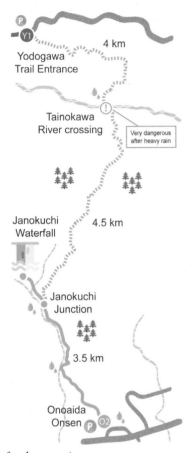

- **To Janokuchi Waterfall** (蛇ノ口滝) If the weather prevents hiking in the central mountains, this trail is a fine alternative. It begins to the right of Onoaida Onsen and gently meanders through the forest for an hour before becoming more challenging the closer you come to the waterfall. After 1½ hours (3½ km) the path splits at **Ja-nokuchi-taki Junction** (蛇ノ口滝分かれ) and then it is a 20 min hike on the branch path to the waterfall. Because of the river crossings care should be taken after heavy rain.

- **To Yodogawa Trail Entrance** (Y1) (淀川登山口) Back at Janokuchi Junction, the main trail continues onwards and steeply upwards. It takes a further 3 hours (4.5 km) to reach **Tainokawa River** (鯛之川). You need to cross the river here and do so with caution as after heavy rain it can be untraversable. In 2003 a guide took a group of 5 hikers across Tainokawa and a flash flood washed 3 of them away to their deaths. It is then another 2½ hours (4 km) to the Yodogawa Trail Entrance (Y1) (淀川登山口).

NAGATA TRAIL　　永田歩道

DIFFICULTY: 😊 😊 😊 😊

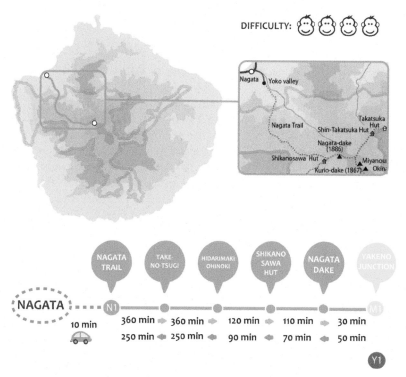

NAGATA

10 min 🚗

NAGATA TRAIL — TAKE-NO-TSUGI — HIDARIMAKI OHINOKI — SHIKANO SAWA HUT — NAGATA DAKE — YAKENO JUNCTION

360 min ➡ 360 min ➡ 120 min ➡ 110 min ➡ 30 min
250 min ⬅ 250 min ⬅ 90 min ⬅ 70 min ⬅ 50 min

CAR: Turn inland just west of Nagata River (永田川) at the gas station. Then take the next left. If you miss it, any one of the roads on the left will take you to the same place. Continue parallel to the river (make sure you do not cross it) and follow the road up for a few minutes. There will be an old weathered sign and a small turning to the left into the Nagata Trail car park.

BUS: Get off at No.1 Nagata (永田) bus stop, keep west of the bridge and walk inland. Turn left to keep parallel to the river and walk for 40 min to reach the car park that marks the start of the trail.

Nagata Trail is very long (12.4 km) and very tough and should only be attempted if you are prepared for the hard slog. Few but the hardiest venture up to or down from Nagata dake this way.

The Trail Entrance is further on from the car park after you have begun the ascent upwards.

Seibu Rindo
Forest Path   NAGATA

Nagata Trail
Entrance

6 km

Take-no-tsuji

5.2 km

Hanayama
Trail

Shikanosawa
hut

1.2 km

1.5 km   Nagata dake
1886m

Water is available at 2 places along the trail both before and after **Take no Tsuji** (竹の辻) which is the first peak, 6 km into the trail.

Shikanosawa Hut (鹿之沢小屋) is waiting at the top for those who do choose this route and after 14 hours

of steep climbing, you probably would collapse with exhaustion at the sight of it. As ever the views are spectacular from **Nagata dake** (永田岳) at 1886 m, which is another 1.2 km or 2 hours up from the hut. But there are of course easier ways to get there! (See the Y1 or M1 trails).

K2 KURIO TRAIL 栗生歩道

DIFFICULTY: 🐵 🐵 🐵 🐵

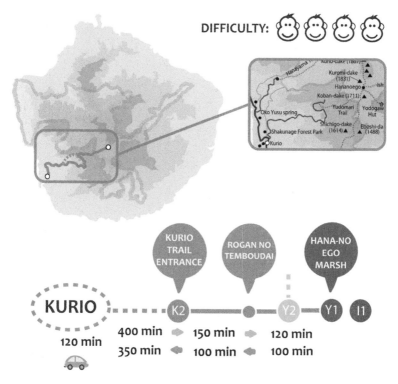

KURIO
TRAIL
ENTRANCE

ROGAN NO
TEMBOUDAI

HANA-NO
EGO
MARSH

KURIO

K2 ———————————— Y2 Y1 I1

400 min ➡ 150 min ➡ 120 min
120 min
350 min ⬅ 100 min ⬅ 100 min

CAR: Turn inland at the traffic signals before you cross Kurio River and
take the Kuromi Forest Path. A whopping 18½ km later (a 2 hour drive
up the rough mountain road) you reach **Kurio Trail Entrance** (栗生歩
道入口). The only obstacle being that there is a gate to prevent cars going
any further than ¾ of the way up.
BUS: Get off at No.127 Kurio-bashi (栗生橋) bus stop and it is a 6½ hour
(18.5 km) walk from Kurio to the trail entrance (5½ to return).

Once you eventually reach the trail entrance (where there is a small
sign to Hana-no-ego Marsh) it is a steady upward climb through thick
forest to **Logan-no-tenboudai** (露岩の展望台) lookout point for 2½
hours (3.5 km). It is then another 2 hour (3 km) ascent to **Hana-no-ego
Marsh** (花之江河) at the crossroads of the main mountain paths.

It is a rarely used trail because of the access problems and the sheer
distances involved between Kurio and the trail entrance. The trail can

however be started much lower down than the actual trail entrance and begins at an altitude of under 400 m on the Kuromi Forest Path. From here it is a steep but fairly straight climb and enables you to avoid the windy road which snakes over the mountain side.

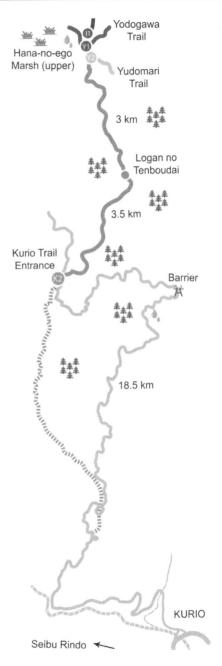

Yodogawa Trail

Hana-no-ego Marsh (upper)

Yudomari Trail

3 km

Logan no Tenboudai

3.5 km

Kurio Trail Entrance

Barrier

18.5 km

KURIO

Seibu Rindo ←

YUDOMARI TRAIL 湯泊歩道

DIFFICULTY:

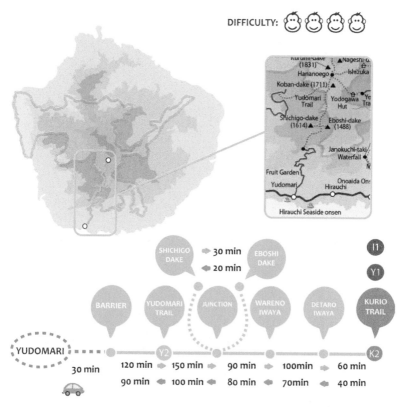

CAR: Take the road inland either side of Yudomari village (湯泊) and keep ascending for around 30 min and eventually there will be a barrier at which point cars are not allowed to cross. The actual start of the trail (湯泊歩道入口) however is considerably further on (2 hours).
BUS: Get off the bus at No.114 Yudomari (湯泊) bus stop. On foot from Yudomari village to the trail head is around 4 hours (10.5 km).

Because this path is so rarely used it is not properly signed and can be in a poor state with objects and overgrowth covering the path. There are also many streams to cross. It is therefore potentially hazardous, especially after heavy rain.

The trail has two branch paths in the following order:

- **Shichigo dake** (七五岳)

  From the entrance to the turn off for Shichigo dake is a 2 hour (3 km) hike along the trail and the summit of Shichigo dake (1488 m) lay a further 30 min (700 m) climb on a side path.

- **Eboshi dake** (烏帽子岳)

  It is only a short walk further on to the second branch on this trail to Eboshi dake (1614 m). The remains of an old hut called **Mino Sansha** (ミノ山舎) marks the turn off and there is a stream for water. The summit of Eboshi dake is a ½ hour (700 m) walk from here.

Back at the main path, if you continue to climb for a further 1½ hours (3 km), you will reach **Wareno Iwaya** (ワレノ岩屋) which has a very basic grotto for up to 4 people but without water source. There are however 2 streams on the way to collect water. Another 1½ hour (3 km) climb after this and there is another grotto called **Detaro Iwaya** (デ゛ータ加ー岩屋). This has enough space for up to 7 people.

There is usually water in the stream nearby but if not 500 m later there is another stream. An hour (1½ km) on from here and the path meets the Kurio Trail (K2) (栗生歩道) as it heads another ½ an hour upwards to **Hana-no-ego Marsh** (花之江河)

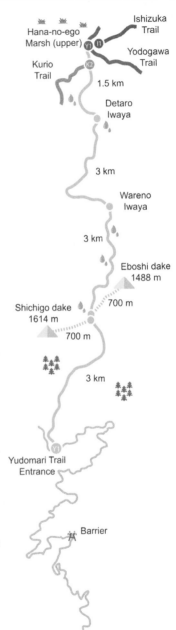

Hana-no-ego Marsh (upper)
Ishizuka Trail
Yodogawa Trail
Kurio Trail
1.5 km
Detaro Iwaya
3 km
Wareno Iwaya
3 km
Eboshi dake
1488 m
700 m
Shichigo dake
1614 m
700 m
3 km
Yudomari Trail Entrance
Barrier

H1 HANAYAMA TRAIL 花山歩道

DIFFICULTY: 😊 😊 😊 😊

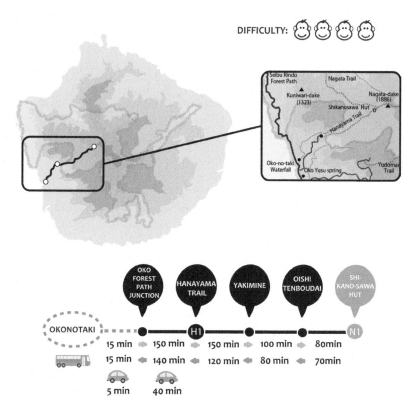

OKONOTAKI

OKO FOREST PATH JUNCTION ⟶ HANAYAMA TRAIL ⟶ YAKIMINE ⟶ OISHI TENBOUDAI ⟶ SHI-KANO-SAWA HUT

15 min ⟹ 150 min ⟹ 150 min ⟹ 100 min ⟹ 80min

15 min ⟸ 140 min ⟸ 120 min ⟸ 80 min ⟸ 70min

5 min   40 min

CAR: To drive up Oko Forest Path you will need a sturdy 4 wheel drive car as the road can be in bad repair in places. It takes around 40 minutes by car to make it to the Hanayama Trail Entrance (花山歩道入口).
BUS: Get off the bus at No.129 Oko-no-taki Waterfall (大川の滝) and walk back for 15 minutes to Oko Forest Path Junction (大川林道分れ). From here it is a 2½ hour walk to the start of the trail.

The attraction of this long trail is that it traverses the virgin forests of the protected Yakushima wilderness area. Fill up with water at the trail entrance and it then takes 2½ hours to climb the 3.8 km to **Yakimine** (焼峰) peak at 1264 m. The trail then levels off for 1 km before rising up a further 1.8 km towards **Oishitenbodai** (大石展望台) lookout point

Shikanosawa Hut

Nagata Trail

2.4 km

Oishitenbodai

2.8 km

Yakimine

5.8 km

Hanayama Trail Entrance

7 km

Okawa River

Oko-no-taki Waterfall

Seibu Rindo Forest Path

Oko Forest Path Junction

and beautiful views of the coast. It then continues to climb, crosses Okawa River 3 times and finally reaches **Shikanosawa Hut** (鹿之沢小屋) and the Nagata Trail (N1) 1½ hours (2.4 km) on from that.

11 WATER ACTIVITIES

SWIMMING

IN THE SEA

The most popular spots to swim in the sea are at:
- **ISSO BEACH** - see ISSO AREA section for more details.
- **HARUTAHAMA** - see ANBO AREA section for more details.
- **KURIO BEACH** - see KURIO AREA section for more details.

In all three beaches safe areas have been designated and have life guards in the summer months (mid-July to end of August).

Note: Be aware that INAKAHAMA BEACH has off-shore currents which run close to the beach so swimming here is not recommended.

IN THE RIVER

The following places are good for swimming in the summer months:
- **MIYANOURA RIVER** at Yakushima Comprehensive Nature Park. See MIYAN-OURA AREA section for more details.
- **NAGATA RIVER** at Yokogawa. See NA-GATA AREA section for more details.
- **ANBO RIVER**. See ANBO AREA section for more details.

SNORKELING

There are many places you can snorkel around Yakushima but the popular (and relatively safe) places with a wide selection of underwater sights are:
- **MOTOURA BAY** (元浦) in Isso. This is the bay east of Isso beach and it is a popular spot with scuba and snorkelling tours.
- **HARUTAHAMA BEACH** in Anbo. Not the swimming area but where the river meets the sea.
- **YUDOMARI PORT**. Head towards the seaside Onsen but when at the water's edge do not turn left to the onsen but continue 500 m

straight on to the end of the road and then walk over the rocks to the right of the harbour wall.
• **TSUKASAKI TIDE POOL** in Kurio but not at low or high tides. You can check the tides with the app at yakumonkey.com/p/tides-in-yakushima.html

Bring or buy a snorkel. You can buy them in any of the stores listed including in Kurio at S-Mart Convenience Store. They can also be rented in some locations like at Ever Blue Yakushima or your accommodation. Some kind of sea footwear is a must and if you are anywhere near rocks wear gloves.

SUP/CANOEING/KAYAKING

Moving along Yakushima's rivers offers rewarding and often stunning views of the forest and mountains. Rental canoes and kayaks are usually available near Anbo River although many companies now prefer to offer guide services. Tourist information centres can often help with reservations.

A 2-3 hour trip in Anbo River with a guide ranges from ¥7,000-¥8,000. To rent a kayak without the guide costs ¥3,000 - ¥5,000 for 1 or ¥5,000 - ¥8,000 for 2 depending if you want ½ day or a full day.
• **GREEN MOUNT** offer half or full day Stand-up Paddle boarding (SUP) tours on Anbo River. You can book directly in English on their website. We tried SUP and SUP yoga on Anbo River and the team were very professional and a lot of fun. It costs ¥8,000 for 1 – but the more people in your group the cheaper the price per person. Web: http://greenmount.jp/english Email: info@greenmount.jp
• **YAKUSHIMA FIELD GUIDE SPINNAKER** (屋久島フィールドガイドスピニカ) is in Anbo and offers full and half day trips on kayaks. Tel: 46-3223 Web: http://yakushima-kayak.com Email: spinnaker@yakushima-kayak.com

SCUBA DIVING

For anyone who has never dived before, there are plenty of companies offering supervised diving with an instructor. Prices range from ¥10,000 – ¥11,000 for ½ day (1 dive) and ¥15,000 – ¥16,000 for a full day (2 dives). Each session lasts around 3 hours but the dive itself is for 30 min and descends to 4 - 6 m under the water. The rest of the time is spent in safety training.

All companies offer a pick-up service from your accommodation and

GREEN
MOUNT

Stand Up Paddling is the best way to explore the clear water in Yakushima. Relax and enjoy cruising on a board. You can also enjoy tea time and do yoga on the water!

Let us take you for an experience you will never forget and see the real Yakushima at its heart!

SUP half-day Tour
SUP early morning Tour
Yoga half-day Tour

include insurance, equipment, tax and a soft drink. For full day trips you need your own lunch. You will need a swimsuit, a change of clothes and shampoo/soap/towel. The tourist information or your accommodation can help organise this or try the following companies:

• **YAKUSHIMA DIVING SERVICE MORI-TO-UMI** (屋久島ダ イビングサービス もりとうみ) also known as **YAKUSHIMA NATURE GUIDE** in Miyanoura offers a variety of dives from absolute beginner upwards. We did a beginner's afternoon dive and the instruction and customer care was excellent. They would really like to do more dives with foreigners and are preparing English materials. Web: http://mori-umi.net or find them on facebook. You can see Shigeru san's photos here: https://www.facebook.com/yakushima.photo Tel: 49-1260.

• **EVER BLUE YAKUSHIMA** (エバーブルー屋久島) in Miyan-oura offers certified PADI training as well as short dives. They also rent scuba and snorkelling equipment. Tel: 42-0505 Web: yakushima-diving.com/eng.html (English) Email: eby@yakushima-diving.com

For experienced divers who just want to rent the equipment. The prices are around ¥500 each for a mask, snorkel, fins and boots (¥2,100 for all), and BC, regulator and wet suit around ¥1,500 each.

12 CRAFT ACTIVITIES

Yakushima is famous for two crafts: its Yakusugi woodcraft and its Yakushimayaki pottery. Both can be bought is many stores on the island but you can also have a go at making them yourself.

YAKUSUGI WOODCRAFT

There are many places on the island where you can, with supervision, make your own objects from yakusugi wood. This could be anything from 45 min to 2 hours depending on what you make. The most common objects are key chains and chopsticks. Here are some of the companies which offer this service:

• **SUGINOYA** (杉の舎本店) is a Yakusugi craft shop in Koseda very close to the airport. You can make chopsticks with yakusugi in about an hour. Book directly at the craft shop. Price: ~ ¥1,500 Tel: 43-5441.

• **TAKEDA KAN** (武田館) is a large shop and workshop on Route 77 in Anbo at the first main intersection (coming from Miyanoura). You can make chopsticks and key chains for ~ ¥1,500 and it takes around 45 min. Tel: 46-2123 Web: www.yakusugi-takeda.com. Book directly at the shop.

If you just want a piece of Yakusugi to take back with you, come to my old workshop. This is one of the oldest on Yakushima and I used to work in that workshop right behind the stack of wood. They work with so much wood that there is often pieces left over and Kashima-san offers them for sale. **KASHIMA KOUGEI** (鹿島工芸) is on the hill leading south out of Anbo on the sea side of the Route 77. There is usually a large pile of wood for sale outside the workshop. All pieces are priced and if no one is there put the money in the container provided.

YAKUSHIMA POTTERY

• **YAKUSHIMAYAKI SHIMPACHINOGAMA** (屋久島焼新八野 [シンパチノ] 窯) is in Hirauchi, is the original 'Yakushima' pottery and

the oldest potter's on the island. They use iron-rich Yakushima clay and bake in a firewood kiln that includes ash and weathered coral to give a unique finish. It offers supervised pottery making by hand ~ ¥2,000 or by potter's wheel ~ ¥2,500 between 15.00-18.30 on Wed, Thurs and Frid. You get to make 4 creations over 1-2 hours and 2 of these can then be glazed. You can then arrange to send on your creations once

dried and glazed to a forwarding address (it takes 2 months!). Book beforehand and English is spoken.

The sign for the pottery is 200 m after the turn off for Hirauchi Seaside Onsen (平内海中温泉) on the mountain side of the main road (heading towards Kurio). By bus get off at No.113 Nishikaikon (西開墾) bus stop and head inland. The pottery is a short distance on the left. TEL 47-2624. Web: http://yakushimayaki.com.

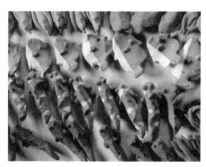

13 MAP OF YAKUSHIMA

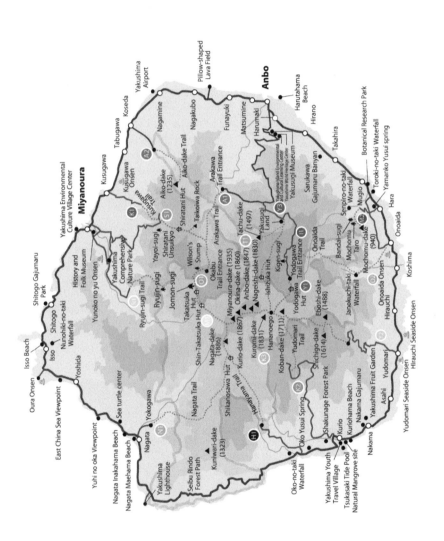

14 Index

CPSIA information can be obtained
at www.ICGtesting.com
Printed in the USA
BVOW05s0145171217
502917BV00027B/170/P

9 780956 150776